S1NGLE ADULTS

Resource and Recipients for

REVIVAL

Dan R. Crawford
COMPILER

BROADMAN PRESS
Nashville, Tennessee

© Copyright 1985 • Broadman Press
All rights reserved
4232-36
ISBN: 0-8054-3236-1

Dewey Decimal Classification: 269.2
Subject Headings: SINGLE PEOPLE // EVANGELISTIC WORK
Library of Congress Catalog Card Number: 85-7889
Printed in the United States of America

Unless otherwise indicated, all Scripture quotations are taken from the *New American Standard Bible.* Copyright © The Lockman Foundation, 1960, 1962, 1963, 1968, 1971, 1972, 1973, 1975, 1977. Used by permission.

Scripture quotations marked KJV are taken from the King James Version of the Bible.

Scripture quotations marked NIV are taken from the HOLY BIBLE *New International Version,* copyright © 1978, New York Bible Society. Used by permission.

Library of Congress Cataloging in Publication Data

Crawford, Dan R., 1941-
  Single adults.

  Bibliography: p. 175
  1. Revivals.   2. Church work with single people.
I. Title.
BV3793.C675 1985   259   85-7889
ISBN 0-8054-3236-1 (pbk.)

Acknowledgments

Compiling a book such as this requires the cooperative effort of many people. Thanks are obviously due to the contributing authors, all of whom donated their time and energies without financial remuneration. Beyond the authors, thanks are due to secretaries who typed manuscripts, families who supported, and probably willing singles who listened to the materials and approved or improved on them.

Thanks are also due the Family Ministry Department of the Baptist Sunday School Board for their support of this book and especially to their former single adult consultant, Ann Alexander Smith, who served as a significant inspiration for the book. All proceeds from this book will be donated to the Ann Alexander Smith Scholarship Fund at Southeastern Baptist Seminary, Wake Forest, North Carolina.

A special thanks to a significant single, Jan Duke, who retyped the various manuscripts, preparing one master manuscript for publication.

DAN R. CRAWFORD

Contributors

Dan R. Crawford is national evangelism consultant with students, singles, and young adults, Specialized Evangelism Department, Home Mission Board of the Southern Baptist Convention, Atlanta, Georgia. He is the author of *EvangeLife: A Guide to Lifestyle Evangelism; First Things First: A Daily Guide for Summer Missionaries;* and *Where One Is Gathered in His Name: A Hundred Days of Singular Servanthood.* He is also the coordinator of "Pressure Points: Issues in Single Adult Lifestyle" published by the Home Mission Board, SBC.

Brian L. Harbour is pastor of First Baptist Church, Pensacola, Florida. He is the author of four books: *Famous Singles of the Bible, Famous Couples of the Bible, Famous Parents of the Bible,* and *From Cover to Cover,* all published by Broadman Press.

R. Philip Roberts was assistant professor of evangelism at The Southern Baptist Theological Seminary, Louisville, Kentucky, when he wrote his chapter. He has now become pastor of International Baptist Church, Brussels, Belgium. He has written numerous articles for publication.

Ed Seabough is director of marketing for V.I.P.—Unique Travel (a Christian travel agency) in Houston, Texas. He is the author of *After the Riot, Babble On, New Day on the Hudson, Sunsets and Ski Trails, So You're Going to College,* and *Youth: A Doctrine of Missions.*

Clay L. Price is director of program research for the Home Mission Board of the Southern Baptist Convention, Atlanta, Georgia.

Milt Hughes is consultant in Bible study and discipleship, National Student Ministries Department, Sunday School Board of the Southern Baptist Convention, Nashville, Tennessee. He is the author of *Spiritual Journey Notebook, Share Seminar Workbook, Being a Christian, Living Discipleship, Patterns for Discipleship,* and material for *Master Plan.*

Donna Christian McConnico is minister with college and single adults, Dawson Memorial Baptist Church, Birmingham, Alabama.

Woody Northcutt is director of singles at Riverside Baptist Church, Denver, Colorado. He is a contributing writer for "Pressure Points I: Issues in the Single Adult Lifestyle" published by the Home Mission Board, SBC.

Gary D. Chapman is associate pastor responsible for adult ministries at Calvary Baptist Church, Winston-Salem, North Carolina. He is the author of *Hope for the Separated, Toward a Growing Marriage,* and *Building Relationships: A Discipleship Program for Married Couples.* Gary is also a contributing writer for "Pressure Points I: Issues in the Single Adult Lifestyle" published by the Home Mission Board, SBC.

Dorothy Johnson Sizemore is dean of students at Meredith College, Raleigh, North Carolina.

J. Clark Hensley is executive director emeritus of the Christian Action Commission of the Mississippi Baptist Convention in Jackson, Mississippi. He is the author of ten books including *Coping with Being Single Again, Help for the Family,* and *Good News for Today's Singles.*

Bob Thrift is director of the counseling ministry, University Baptist Church, Coral Gables, Florida. He is the author of *The Ball Park.*

Randy Gallaway is director of the Baptist Student Union at California Baptist College and area Baptist student director for the Riverside area of California. He is a frequent contributor to *The Student,* published by the Sunday School Board, SBC.

Ken Morris, Jr., is administrative pastor, Near North Baptist Church, Chicago, Illinois. Ken was instrumental in the beginning of this church in the condominium complex (Sandburg Terrace) where he lives. He is a contributing writer to "Pressure Points II: Issues in the Single Adult Lifestyle" published by the Home Mission Board, SBC.

Milton O. Tyler is installation staff chaplain, Neubrucke Air Force Base, Germany. He has written "Do They Really Get the

Message?" for *Proclaim,* published by the Sunday School Board, SBC.

Horace L. Kerr is supervisor, Senior Adult and Single Adult Section, Family Ministry Department, Sunday School Board of the Southern Baptist Convention, Nashville, Tennessee. He is the author of *How to Minister to Senior Adults in Your Church* (Broadman Press) and of a chapter in *Unto a Ripe Old Age* (Convention Press).

Joyce Ashcraft is director, Baptist Student Union at Rice University and the Texas Medical Center, Houston, Texas. She also served as chairperson and contributing writer for "Pressure Points II: Issues in Single Adult Lifestyle" published by the Home Mission Board, SBC.

Herman Rios is national evangelism consultant with ethnics, Specialized Evangelism Department, Home Mission Board of the Southern Baptist Convention, Atlanta, Georgia. He is the author of *Intercessory Praying Guide.*

Barbara McNeir is minister of single adults, Columbia Baptist Church, Falls Church, Virginia. She is a contributing writer to "Pressure Points I: Issues in the Single Adult Lifestyle" published by the Home Mission Board, SBC.

Timothy M. Larkin is director of the counseling ministry, Uptown Baptist Church, Chicago, Illinois.

Mike Clayton is program administrator and single adult minister, First Southern Baptist Church in Del City, Oklahoma. He is the author of *Single Adult Ministry: Practical Tools for the Local Church.*

Paul Griffin Jones, II, is executive director-treasurer, Christian Action Commission of the Mississippi Baptist Convention, Jackson, Mississippi. He is the author of *The Bible Speaks on Sex, Love, and Marriage* and *Maternal Child Care: A Strategy for the Future.*

Ralph E. Hunt is associate pastor for evangelism and singles, Eastside Baptist Church, Marietta, Georgia.

Charles B. Baker is pastor, First Baptist Church, Ada, Oklahoma. He is the author of *It's My World* and a contributing writer to "Pressure Points I: Issues in the Single Adult Lifestyle" published by the Home Mission Board, SBC.

David Roddy is minister to single adults, First Baptist Church, Dallas, Texas. He is the author of *How to Develop a Caring Sunday*

School. He is also a contributing writer to *Working with Single Adults in Sunday School* and has written numerous articles for *Christian Single* and *Church Growth of America.*

Larry Golden is campus minister/administrator of the Baptist Student Union, University of Missouri, Columbia, Missouri.

H. Paul Royal is minister with single adults, Park Cities Baptist Church, Dallas, Texas. He is a contributing writer to "Pressure Points I: Issues in the Single Adult Lifestyle" published by the Home Mission Board, SBC.

Bill Myers is minister to singles and students, First Baptist Church, San Antonio, Texas. He is the author of *Myers Mexican Food.*

Gene Bolin is pastor, Metro Baptist Church, Manhattan Island, New York City. He is the author of *Christian Witness on Campus.*

Joey Hancock is pastor, Ash Street Baptist Church, Forest Park, Georgia.

Donna H. Poynor is minister of single adults and administration, First Baptist Church, Gainesville, Florida.

Deborah Anne Murrell is minister to single adults, First Baptist Church, Temple Terrace, Florida. She has written articles for *Christian Single,* published by the Sunday School Board, SBC.

Tim Cleary is single adult consultant, Family Ministry Department, Sunday School Board of the Southern Baptist Convention, Nashville, Tennessee.

Billy Justiss was minister to singles and properties administrator, Two Rivers Baptist Church, Nashville, Tennessee, when he wrote his chapter. He is now minister of education and administration, Sagamore Hills Baptist Church, Fort Worth, Texas.

F. Maurine Freeze is business administrator, Arkansas Digestive Diseases Clinic, Little Rock, Arkansas.

Rennie Berry is director of evangelism, Kansas-Nebraska Convention of Southern Baptists, Topeka, Kansas. He is responsible for the single adult ministry in the Kansas-Nebraska Convention.

William G. Tanner is president, Home Mission Board of the Southern Baptist Convention, Atlanta, Georgia. He is a contributing writer to numerous periodicals and is the author of *Hurry Before Sundown: The Urgency of Evangelizing Our Nation* (Broadman Press).

Contents

Introduction

The next time you go home to your family, ask yourself how many of your co-workers and business contacts have gone home to lonely apartments or empty-feeling houses.

The next time the teller behind the bank window tells you to have a good day, ask yourself if he could be one of over thirty-five million single adults in this country who never married.

The next time you honk your car horn at a stranger, ask yourself if that person could be one of the millions of Americans who find themselves separated from their mate—not yet single; not fully married.

The next time you pass a health club or physical fitness center, ask yourself if the person coming out of the door could be one of over one million single adults who divorced last year.

The next time you see someone eating alone in a restaurant, ask yourself if that person could be one of over two million single adults who experienced the death of a mate last year.

The next time you drive around your neighborhood looking at five recently purchased houses, ask yourself if one was purchased by a single adult. If your neighborhood is a cross section of the country, one in every five houses sold last year was sold to a single adult.

The next time you watch five children at play, ask yourself if one of them lives in a single-parent household. If your area is a cross section of our nation, one in every five children under age eighteen lives with a single parent.

The next time you shake hands with ten adults in your church, ask yourself if four of them are single. If your church is reaching a cross section of your community, your church will have four single adults for every six married adults.

Single adults are no longer a separate segment of society; they are part of the fabric of our nation, our communities, our school systems, our businesses, our leisure activities, and our churches. They can no longer be stereotyped, for they are all of us. *Singles: The New Americans* is a "nationally representative study revealing how single men and women in America conduct their private lives."[1] While some of the contents of the book are questionable, the title is exactly accurate. Single adults are "the new Americans."

A friend recently asked me, "How do you reach single adults?" My answer was, "How do you reach people?" There are no easy answers; there are no stereotyped programs, for singles are people with the same needs, hurts, and feelings as the rest of society, plus some unique ones of their own.

This book is an attempt to not only help you understand single adults better but, hopefully, to reach out to them with greater ease and effectiveness.

When I moved my family to Georgia several years ago, we decided to have a house built for us. We chose a lot and found a builder. We chose a house plan that the builder had built on other lots. We made our adjustments to his plan and the construction began. When construction was completed, we moved in. Six months later, when the spring rains came to Georgia, a four-inch rain invaded our house. With eight inches of water standing on our floor, we made a significant observation. Although there was nothing wrong with our plan and basically nothing wrong with the lot that could not be corrected, the house plan we selected should not have been built on this lot. With a few adjustments and a new approach or two, this predesigned house plan could have fit, and we would have lived happily ever after. As it was, we endured three lawsuits and eighteen months of legal proceedings to correct a mistake.

This is a book of plans, of designs, of ideas. No one plan or design or idea will fit all situations. The book is not intended to be a blueprint for your singles ministry. It is designed to offer insight, provide motivation, further understanding, and, hopefully, enhance revival.

To accomplish this, a diversity of authors was recruited. Among the contributing authors, five are never-married single adults, three have been divorced, two have been widowed, and two are remarried. The remainder are married, some marrying later in life than the average, thus spending significant years as single adults. Among the authors, eleven are ministers with single adults on local church staffs, while six others are denominational workers with single adults as a part of their job description. Five of the authors work with college-age single adults. Other types of ministry represented by the contributing authors include: pastor, seminary professor, layperson, associate pastor, college administrator, counselor, chaplain, denominational worker, and missionary. Diversity of authorship is further seen in the fact that authors represent ministry in eighteen states and one foreign country with seven authors serving as denominational workers with nationwide responsibilities.

In the midst of diversity, you will find several commonalities. All authors felt the pressure of limited space to develop their subject. Each author could have written much more. Were you to communicate with any one of them, he or she would no doubt be happy to share further ideas and materials with you.

Perhaps the greatest commonality is the belief that single adults will be reached best when single adults are used in the reaching. The focus of E-1 evangelism, which "evangelizes people in one's own language and culture"[2] must be narrowed even more. Within language and culture, the best evangelism is done among people with common life situations.

Therefore, the best vehicle for communicating the good news of Jesus Christ to a twenty-eight-year-old, never-married, non-Christian male is a twenty-eight-year-old, never-married, Christian male. The best vehicle for communicating the good news to a thirty-six-year-old, non-Christian divorced mother of two children is a thirty-six-year-old, Christian divorced mother of two children. The best vehicle for communicating the good news to a fifty-three-year-old non-Christian widow is a fifty-three-year-old Christian widow. While in each of these cases the life situations are similar, the Christians have found an inner resource in Jesus Christ to help them cope with the situation. It is that resource that Christian singles must share with their peers.

Running rampant in Christian circles, especially single circles, is the idea that one must reach a certain spiritual level before communicating the good news to a nonbeliever. It is almost as if we had a scale of spirituality from 1 to 10, with 1 being conversion and 10 being perfection. Many singles feel they must be at least a 7 to witness. Events in their lives or the lack of events in their lives have been labeled by the world as failures. Often, too often, the label is transferred from the event or lack of event (divorce, separation, no wedding, etc.) to the person, and they begin to see themselves as failures. With that kind of self-image, the natural conclusion is an inadequate life-style for Christian witness.

I have told in another book of my experience with a pastor who, in a strategy planning meeting, asked me, "How can you have the audacity to train single adults to witness when they have so many problems of their own?" I responded that Jesus had problems and proceeded to name twelve for him who followed Jesus around for most of three years.[3]

Where on your spiritual scale would you place disciples who, in the hour of great need, betrayed, denied, cut off ears, ran off naked, deserted, etc.? Jesus got them together later and said to them, "*You* shall be My witnesses" (Acts 1:8, author's italics). Jesus is not looking for perfect "10's" and neither should we. Single adults, whether they see themselves as "1's" or "10's," must be faithful witnesses to all people but especially to other singles. God does not disown a person when down or defeated or discouraged or dismayed or divorced. We are all still His witnesses.

In his book *The Wounded Healer,* Henri J. M. Nouwen captured both the frustration of singleness and the challenge to the church when he wrote, "No man can stay alive when nobody is waiting for him. Everyone who returns from a long and difficult trip is looking for someone waiting for him at the station or the airport. Everyone wants to tell his story and share his moments of pain and exhilaration with someone who stayed home, waiting for him to come back."[4]

The church must become a listening friend, where singles can tell their story, share their moments of pain and exhilaration, and dream new dreams in the presence of supportive concern. But more than this, the church must so implant the good news of

Jesus Christ within single adults that He becomes a significant part of their story, shared with other single adults.

Thus, here is a book to motivate singles in evangelism and to encourage those who work with singles to view them not as only recipients of the good news, but also as resource for revival.

DAN R. CRAWFORD

1. Jacqueline Simenauer and David Carroll, ed., *Singles: The New Americans* (New York: Simon and Schuster, 1982), p. 7.

2. J. D. Douglas, Ed., *Let the Earth Hear His Voice,* International Congress on World Evangelization (Minneapolis: Worldwide Publications, 1975), p. 104.

3. Dan R. Crawford, *EvangeLife: A Guide to Life-style Evangelism* (Nashville: Broadman Press, 1984), p. 69.

4. Henri J. M. Nouwen, *The Wounded Healer* (Garden City, NY: Doubleday & Company, 1972), p. 66.

Part I
Roles of Single Adults

1
Single Adults in the Bible
BRIAN L. HARBOUR

An older single prepared a will in which she left the following instructions: "When I die and am buried, do not put 'Miss' on my tombstone for I have not missed anything important in life!" A growing number of singles are reaching the conclusion that a husband or wife is not a requirement for happiness. Instead, they are satisfied being single. Singleness is not a temporary state from which they hope soon to be delivered. Rather, singleness is a viable permanent life-style for the Christian.

Does the Bible speak to this matter? Yes, it does. In the Bible are many single adults who played significant roles in the movement of redemptive history. For some, singleness was a temporary state preceding marriage or following the dissolution of marriage by death or divorce. Hagar (Gen. 21), Naomi (Ruth), and Anna (Luke 2:36-38) are prime examples. For others, singleness was a permanent life-style. Miriam (Ex. 2:4; 15:20-21), John the Baptizer (John 1:6-9,15-37), and Paul (Phil. 4:11; 1 Cor. 7) are prime examples.

What role did these singles play in the Bible?

The Problems of Singles

These biblical singles reflect many of the same problems which singles face today.

Rejection. Hagar (Gen. 21) experienced the common problem

of rejection. Hagar was a victim of another woman's jealousy and of a man too weak to stand up for the right. Like her modern-day counterparts, she was tossed aside. Read the story in Genesis 21 to sense the anger, the ego deflation, and the loneliness which invaded her life following her rejection.

How did Hagar deal with her rejection? She found help from two directions.

In the midst of her sorrow, she called on God. When she did, she saw what she had not seen before, a well of water from which to receive nourishment (Gen. 21:19). That is more than a factual part of Hagar's story. It is a paradigm of our experience today. Rejection evolves from anger to depression because our focus is on ourselves. From that perspective, no way out seems to be available. However, when we dare to focus on God, our perspective changes. Now we see what we did not see before, a well of water in God from whose stream we can be spiritually revived.

Hagar's responsibility for her son, Ishmael, also sparked recovery. God reminded her that Ishmael's future was in her hands. Likewise, when rejection comes to you, your life is not over; nor do your responsibilities end. Do you have children? They are your responsibility. Do you have a job? Then commit yourself to it with new fervor. What about you? You are still responsible for how you react to the things that happened. Rejection does not remove you from the resources of God.

Rebellion. Dinah (Gen. 34) illustrates another problem which singles have to deal with today: rebellion. The biblical writer declares the nature of the problem in Genesis 34:1. "Dinah . . . went out to visit the daughters of the land." Who were the daughters of the land? They were the pagan people who inhabited the land. Dinah was not a part of the pagan people of the land. She was a descendant of Abraham to whom God had given special promises. The tragedy of Dinah's life is that she opted to become a part of the daughters of the land rather than to remain as a part of the people of God.

Like Dinah, many singles today reject their spiritual heritage as children of God and promenade into permissiveness. While living in the world, they choose to become a part of the world. Why?

Some commentators suggest that restlessness was Dinah's motive. Life was dull and empty. The simple nomadic life of her father had become boring. She wanted excitement. The thrill of the outside world appealed to her. Boredom demanding stimulation, emptiness craving fulfillment—those were the motives that drove Dinah out of her father's house.

Other commentators suggest that she was motivated by the restrictions of her home and the desire for freedom. She wanted to get away from parental control so she could do all the things that she fantasized and dreamed about.

Many singles today are hot on Dinah's trail. Driven by a desire for excitement and freedom, they rebel against their spiritual heritage. Read the rest of Dinah's story. The message of the story is repeated throughout God's Word: excitement and freedom are not found by visiting the daughters of the land but by living in fellowship with the Father.

Remorse. Naomi (Ruth) is a prime example of yet another problem of singles: the remorse which comes with the loss of a mate through death. No other experience of life is more traumatic than that. Naomi reflected the full measure of sorrow caused by the impact of death (Ruth 1:5,11,13,20-21).

The death of a mate ushers in a status change which is often accompanied by an identity crisis. "We" language is no longer appropriate. Yet it was in that "we-ness" that the person's identity may have been centered. Now a new search has to be initiated to determine who we are and what we are to do with our lives.

For the Christian, stability comes in the promise of One who faced death, won the victory over it, and shares that victory with us. Jesus reminds us that death is not the period at the end of the sentence of life but a comma, introducing a new stage of life. Jesus reminds us that we who believe never say good-bye for the last time.

Hope also comes in the reminder that God still has plans for our life. The death of a spouse does not mark the end of life for you. Sometimes life after the death of a spouse can be a life of deeper and fuller service for God. (For example, read about Anna in Luke 2:36-38.) Or life after the death of a spouse can be a time for building a new relationship. (For example, read about Ruth, Naomi's daughter-in-law, in the Book of Ruth.) In either case, the death of a mate does not mark the end of life for the survivor—simply a change in life.

The Possibility for Singles

These biblical singles also demonstrate in their lives the possibilities open to singles in God's kingdom, both in biblical times and today.

Service. Miriam (Ex. 15:20-21) is a beautiful example of a single who served God. Miriam was no minor character in the unfolding drama of Hebrew history. On the contrary, she was a key figure whose story is woven together inextricably with the story of her two brothers, Moses and Aaron.

Miriam served her nation. Eugenia Price calls her "the first woman patriot mentioned in the Bible."[1] Exodus 15:20-21 shows Miriam in a position of responsibility over the Hebrew women. In a critical time in Hebrew history, Miriam willingly filled her place of responsibility. Single adults today should also play an important part in keeping our nation strong.

In addition, Miriam served her God. The Bible calls her a "prophetess" (Ex. 15:20). The word connotes one who was inspired and directed to teach the will of God. She was not only involved in leading the people, but also in worshiping God. Today doors are opening for singles in the church. As never before, singles have a chance to be the church too, as they serve the Lord through His church.

Satisfaction. Paul (1 Cor. 7; Phil. 4:11) is a biblical example of a single who found satisfaction in his single status. Paul did not bemoan his singleness. Instead, he exalted it because it provided freedom to serve God more fully (1 Cor. 7:32-35).

Why was Paul content in his singleness? Several reasons emerge from his experience.

Paul was a satisfied single because he put marriage in the proper perspective. He realized marriage was not for everyone.

Paul was a satisfied single because he developed other meaningful relationships. The relationship hunger, inherent in human life, was satisfied through comradeship with friends instead of companionship with a mate.

Paul was a satisfied single because he put his life in God's hands. The key to your contentment as a person is not your marital status but whether you have turned your life over to God. Paul put Christ first (Phil. 1:21). In the end, that is why he could say, "[Married or single], I have learned to be content in whatever circumstances I am" (Phil. 4:11).

Singleness is not simply a modern-day phenomenon. Singles in biblical days faced the same problems and had the same possibilities as single adults today. The role of single adults in the Bible can help you fulfill your role as God's single in today's world.

---

1. Eugenia Price, *The Unique World of Women* (Grand Rapids, Mich.: Zondervan Publishing House, 1969), p. 38.

2

Single Adults in Spiritual Awakenings

R. PHILIP ROBERTS

"But I want you to be free from concern. One who is unmarried is concerned about the things of the Lord, how he may please the Lord" (1 Cor. 7:32).

The history of single adults in the movements of revival is both rich and variegated. Singles have often played a leading role in being the instruments of God in both initiating movements of renewal and in seeing them through to become world-changing spiritual reformations.

There is very little historical or sociological data available on the place of single adults in awakenings prior to the eighteenth century. Of course, we have the known biblical examples of Paul's apparent singleness (1 Cor. 7:8), of several of the Old Testament figures being used of God in their youth and singleness—Joseph, David, and Daniel among others.

By the twelfth century, celibacy was imposed on the clergy of the Roman Catholic Church. Consequently, both in the pre-Reformation movements of spiritual renewal and in a good part of the sixteenth-century Protestant Reformation itself, most of the leaders of the awakening were single. Francis of Assisi (1182-1226), Girolamo Savonarola (1452-1498), John Wycliff (c. 1329-

1384), Geert Groote (1340-1384), and John Hus (1373-1415) all exercised significant roles in serving to arouse Christians to a higher level of devotion and piety. Many of their followers were also single.

Francis encouraged Christian devotion and charity to the poor. He undertook evangelistic missions to Syria in 1212 and Morocco in 1213-1214. Peter Waldo revived interest in reading the Bible and directing new circles of Christians by strict biblical guidelines. Savonarola's forthright and fiery biblical expositions in Florence stirred and moved that city to new levels of seriousness. John Wycliff translated and circulated parts of the Bible throughout England. As the "Morning Star of the Reformation," he encouraged a lay preacher's movement called the Lollards. Geert Groote began in the Netherlands the renewal movement "Brethren of the Common Life"; and John Hus, as a celibate priest, stirred Bohemia by questioning much of the church's traditional and nonbiblical practices.

The Protestant Reformation of the sixteenth century restored the priority of biblical authority and emphasis on salvation by God's grace through faith. Subsequently, the Reformation induced genuine spiritual interest and vitality in the lives of numerous people. The prime mover of theological and spiritual transformation was an unmarried professor of theology at Wittenburg University—Martin Luther (1483-1546). He was not married until he was forty-two, well after the Reformation was under way. His wife, Katherina von Bora, was an exnun who shared his religious views. She was a woman of great earnestness and strength. Because she was married to Luther, both of those elements of her personality were severely tested—not to mention her patience!

The Reformation destroyed the notion of manditory celibacy for Protestant pastors and theologians. However, the rich contribution of singles to spiritual renewal continued.

In the eighteenth century spiritual revival swept North America, England, and parts of Central Europe. Up until that time the Evangelical/Protestant church was primarily concerned with carrying out the theological and ecclesiastical implications of the sixteenth-century Reformation. Denominations which evolved from Luther's revolt and the return to biblical patterns of church structure were primarily preoccupied with establishing ideal congregations and churches.

The Great Awakening in America, the Evangelical/Methodist Revival in England, and the Moravian Movement on the European continent altered that perspective. By the end of the 1700s, although Christians were still concerned with being as biblical as possible in the direction of church life and thought, evangelism had become an increased concern. Spreading the gospel had moved significantly up the church's list of priorities. Consequently, the church (Baptists included) moved into the nineteenth century and made it the greatest period of missionary expansion and evangelism since the early church.

Significantly, single adults played very important roles in both the eighteenth- and nineteenth-century movements of renewal. In New England a young Christian student at Yale, David Brainerd (1718-1747), was expelled for "intemperate, indiscreet zeal." His compassion was kindled for the salvation of New England Indians. This concern moved him not only to share the gospel with them but to dedicate himself to long hours of concentrated prayer for their salvation. Sometimes he was known to have lain prostrate in snowy, wintry fields as he interceded for them.

Brainerd was engaged to one of the daughters of Jonathan Edwards, the renowned Puritan divine. But Brainerd died of tuberculosis before their marriage. So impressed was Edwards with Brainerd's spirituality that he had the young man's diary published. *The Journal of David Brainerd* was subsequently widely read. It finally found its way to Northamptonshire in England and was read by a young Baptist—William Carey. Brainerd's obvious and deep commitment to evangelism fanned the flame of Carey's devotion and contributed to his becoming the first English Baptist overseas missionary.

In England the Methodist or Evangelical Revival began and was carried forward on the shoulders of single adults. George Whitefield, 1714-1770, was completing his studies at Oxford University when in 1735 he experienced conversion. Whitefield was the "Trumpet Voice" of the Revival movement, its most powerful preacher. He traversed Britain and colonial America for six years before he was wed. Even then he lived like a single adult, often to the detriment of his marriage. Notably he felt that the "sacred end of marriage" was for husband and wife "to be helpers of each other in the great things of God."[1] He did not consent to matrimony until he had felt that could be true with his beloved.

This same attitude was reflected in the more famous pair of revivalists—Charles and John Wesley. Charles (1707-1788), the poet of revival, married much younger than his brother—in the year 1749. John Wesley married in 1751, at age forty-eight. Charles Wesley's good married life was said to be the reason why he became a much less-traveled evangelist.[2]

John Wesley criticized such behavior—"I cannot understand how a Methodist preacher can answer it to God to preach one sermon or travel one day less in a married state than in a single state."[3] In fact, he struggled hard, on more than one occasion, with the decision of whether to marry. John Wesley also spent much time counseling singles on the subject. In 1743 he even published a tract on the subject— *Thoughts on Marriage and a Single Life*. Its contents are interesting, insightful, and biblical. He is very clear about honoring and not forbidding marriage. Simultaneously, he elucidated the advantages of singleness when the freedom of that state is devoted to God: "You have leisure to improve yourself . . . to wait upon God . . . and to do good to your neighbour in various ways."

Instead of being remorseful about a failed marriage or fretting about finding the right spouse, he encouraged thanksgiving and stewardship of the single state—"Pray constantly and fervently . . . that God would teach you to set a value upon them. And let it be a matter of daily thanksgiving to God, that he has made you a partaker of these benefits."[4]

There were other notable figures in that period who as single adults served God significantly.

Lady Selina, the Countess of Huntingdon (1707-1791), was the wealthy widowed benefactor of evangelicalism. After the death of her husband, she contributed generously to the cause of building evangelical chapels up and down England. George Whitefield was one of her "chaplains" as she underwrote some of his support.

The nineteenth century has been called the "Great Missionary Century" because of the prodigious advancement of the gospel in foreign lands in that period. Much of the mission enterprise was carried forth on the shoulders of single adults. Space fails us here to tell the stories of Lottie Moon, Hudson Taylor, Henry Martyn, and others who gave of themselves in evangelism and spiritual awakening.[5]

Into the twentieth century, the history of revivals bears witness to the importance and place of single adults in the gospel cause. Evan Roberts was a twenty-six-year-old Bible school dropout when God used him in Wales in 1904.[6] The student evangelistic movements and revivals of the 1900s are examples of God's continued use of the unmarried.[7] There is a wealth of heritage and history to this day of the significant roles that singles have played in awakenings.

Conclusion

There are several principles which can be drawn from this brief study. First of all, because spiritual usefulness is not necessarily based on natural ability or on other human qualifications, God uses anyone who makes himself available to Him. Because of certain natural advantages of singles, however, God has often used them in ways and in locales where married persons may not have ventured. Simply the freer, more mobile, and less cluttered life-style of singles has often made them more responsive to the call of God. To say so is not to belittle the marriage state (an unscriptural notion—Heb. 13:4). It is also not to uphold celibacy for celibacy's sake. As the history of revivals has proved, however, God's work can often be done more speedily by those less inhibited by other responsibilities.

Secondly, singleness, following Wesley's advice, is something for which to be thankful and of which to take advantage for the work of building God's kingdom on earth. Such a positive attitude towards its use can help singles to be more responsive to the needs of others and the work of the church.

Thirdly, the history of revivals has shown us that God does not work in a vacuum. If singles are going to continue to be used of God in these significant ways, attention needs to be directed toward them in training for discipleship and evangelism. David Brainerd might not have made a great impact on the life of the church if Jonathan Edwards had not spent the time encouraging and teaching him. Where God is working, others are at work also!

1. George Whitefield, *Letters, 1734-1742* (Edinburgh: Banner of Truth reprint edition, 1976), p. 282.
2. Michael R. Watts, *The Dissenters* (Oxford: Oxford University Press, 1978), p. 421.
3. John Wesley, *Journal* (London: Epworth Press, standard edition, 1938), vol. 3, p. 517.
4. John Wesley, *Works* (New York: Lane and Scott, American edition, 1850), vol. 6, p. 541.
5. For details on the lives of these various personalities, see a helpful church dictionary such as *The Oxford Dictionary of the Christian Church* or *The New International Dictionary of the Christian Church.*
6. See Eifion Evans, *The Welsh Revival of 1904* (Bridgend, Wales: The Evangelical Press of Wales, 1964).
7. See, for instance, J. Edwin Orr's *Campus Aflame* (Glendale, CA: Regal Books, 1971).

3

Single Adults in Modern Society

ED SEABOUGH

Today's single adult *reads: People, The Wall Street Journal, Time, Newsweek, Playboy, Playgirl, The National Inquirer, The Life and Hard Times of Heidi Abramowitz, Prince of Peace, Loving Each Other, The Bridge Across Forever, Men and Women: How Different Are They?, Dr. Burns' Prescription for Happiness, Even Cowgirls Get the Blues, Women Coming of Age, Come Love a Stranger, Changes, Vogue,* and *Gentlemen's Quarterly.*

Today's single adult *wears* clothes designed by: Ralph Lauren, Perry Ellis, Cheryl Tiegs, Lagerfeld, Yves St. Laurent, Albert Nippon, Liz Claiborne, Gloria Vanderbilt, La Coste, Polo, L. L. Bean, Le Baron, Brooks Brothers, Austin Reed, Halston, Donald Brooks, Pierre Cardin, Damon, London Fog, and Jos. A. Banks.

Today's single adult *goes to* movies, concerts, bars, dramas, football games, divorce recovery groups, church, laundromats,

country-western clubs, barbecues, weekend retreats, PTA, ortho-
dontists, banks, shopping, and the credit union.

Today's single adult *saves money* for: a week of skiing at Vail or
Aspen, a Carnival Cruise in the Caribbean, a Club Med Singles
Holiday, a mink jacket, a new sofa, contact lenses, and a VCR.

Today's single adult *dreams* of a Volvo while driving a Honda;
dreams of a Rolex while wearing a Timex; dreams of financial
independence while saving five dollars a week; dreams of a two-
story colonial while living in an efficiency apartment.

Today's single adult is vastly different from the single adult of
ten years ago. According to the Census Bureau, 38 percent of the
nation's twenty- to forty-four-year-olds are single today. That is
34 million people, about twice as many as ten years ago. Whereas
ten years ago "Singleness" was considered a temporary condition on the way to "Marriage" or "Between Marriages," today
"Singleness" is considered an established life-style in and of
itself.

There are basically three categories of today's singles:
  (1) Those who choose to be single,
  (2) Those who want to remain single for a while longer and
      eventually marry,
  (3) Those who want to marry as soon as possible.

In the early 1970s, journalists and TV commentators reported
on "The Single Adult Phenomenon in America." They described
the single adult as living life in the "fast lane," rushing off to the
singles bar every night, hoping to meet someone for a "relationship" even for just one night.

Single adults in the 1980s are generally happy with their lives.
The fact that singleness is an accepted, important part of society
seems to have caused the masses of singles to feel less panicky
about their future. Being single and liking it is becoming more
common and acceptable. A recent issue of *USA Today* nationwide
poll indicates that 52 percent of all singles think their social life
has improved—a significantly higher percentage than improve-
ments in social life cited by married people.

In the 1970s, singles flocked to singles bars in a desperate
search for *someone.* Although the singles bars are still an important
social contact for singles, they now go there to be with friends
rather than to find *someone.* Singles are now finding new ways to

meet each other: places like church, health clubs, supermarkets, jogging, aerobics classes, and self-service laundries.

The health clubs, spas, racquetball courts, jogging trails, and aerobics classes are the singles bars of the 1980s. Fitness is "in" for singles, and it is a great way to meet someone. With the concern for physical well-being there is also a concern for healthier relationships.

Living together without benefit of clergy is still around, but the numbers of "living together" couples are decreasing. Herpes and other sexually transmitted diseases have caused numerous singles to return to a more responsible sexuality.

The single adult culture in America was new when we began our single adult ministries in our churches in the early 70s. Programs were designed by our churches to attract large numbers of singles. Not only were single adults a phenomenon in our culture —a single adult *ministry* in churches was a phenomenon.

In the 1970s we used the words *single adult* in a brochure or a newspaper ad, opened the doors, and watched hordes of singles pour in. Just being together seemed to be enough. Being in church rather than a singles bar became the "in" activity.

In most cities one church became the singles haven. Then other churches caught on. Singles ministries proliferated, and singles discovered "if you can't find that *someone* in church 'A,' go to church 'B,' 'C,' or 'D.' " And as the years progressed we have watched as singles moved en masse from one church to another.

The nature of the single adult in American culture has changed. The single adult is now a full-fledged, 100 percent member of society who need make no apology for his or her life-style. Loneliness, despair, hopelessness, and panic have given way to an intelligent search for personhood.

Therefore, if a church is to do more than just have a *singles group* it must consider outreach, witness, and a creative ministry to the single adult of the 1980s. This means that programs from the 70s are the beginning, but only the beginning. It means that much time should be spent in prayer asking for divine wisdom to:

   (1) determine the needs of single adults in your city,
   (2) discover ways of meeting the needs of the single adults in your city.

My suggestion of a place to begin is to look at who the single adult of today is. What and where does the single adult of today buy—see—watch—like—read—wear—go—dream of? Continue your search for knowledge about single adults by looking at single adults inside and outside the church. If the single adult in American society is to be reached with the gospel of Jesus Christ, we must know not only the gospel but who the single adult is who needs that gospel.

4

Singles in the Future

CLAY L. PRICE

From 1974 to 1983 the number of single adults in the United States increased 44 percent, while the number of married persons increased only 7 percent.[1] What factors prompted the tremendous growth rate of this population segment, and how will recent trends influence the future role of singles in church and society? This chapter examines the current demographic profile of singles, projects trends to 1990, and offers implications for churches.

Current Profile and Recent Trends

In 1983 there were 167 million persons age eighteen and over in the United States: 64.5 million were single and 102.5 million were married. Singles represented 39 percent of the adult population or four of every ten adults. The singles population included 35.9 million never-married persons, 15.8 million divorced or separated persons, and 12.8 million widowed persons.[2]

The marital group with the largest numerical growth during the past ten years has been adults who have never married. Young adults aged eighteen to thirty-four make up 84 percent of the never-married population. From 1974 to 1983 the number of these young, never-married persons increased 11.3 million; in contrast, the number of all married persons increased 7 million.[3]

Factors contributing to the increase in never marrieds were the aging of the baby boom population and the postponement of marriage by young adults. The peak years of the post-World War II baby boom were 1954 to 1964 when over four million births were recorded annually.[4] In 1974 these persons were entering adulthood; by 1983, they were twenty to thirty years old, swelling the ranks of young adults and leading to the increase in number of never marrieds. The second factor, postponement of marriage, occurred as young adults chose to complete their educations and enter the labor force before marrying.[5] This second factor is expected to continue to influence the marital patterns of young adults.

The fastest growing marital group since 1974 has been divorced and separated persons. From 1974 to 1983 the number of singles emerging from broken marriages increased 71 percent. The net gain in divorced/separated persons almost equaled the net gain in number of married persons. Also, the increase in this group has been so great that in 1979 the number of divorced and separated persons exceeded the number of widowed persons for the first time.[6]

Almost one-half of the singles who were divorced or separated in 1983 were thirty-five to fifty-four years old; one-third were twenty-five to thirty-four years old. Factors contributing to divorce continue to include women's labor force participation, decline in family size, changes in marital laws, and less tolerance of marital problems.[7]

The final segment in the same demographic profile of single adults is widowed persons. Although the number of widowed persons increased 1.2 million from 1974 to 1983, their proportion of the adult population has actually declined as the baby boom population has entered adulthood. One of every four singles was a widowed person in 1974; by 1983 their proportion had dropped to one in five.[8] Widowed persons are found in all age groups; however, women age fifty-five and over comprise three-fourths of all widowed persons.

Religious Characteristics of Singles

Of key importance to churches is the role of religion in the lives of single adults. The annual Gallup poll on religion in America includes marital status as a variable in analyzing religious trends.

According to Gallup, the religious participation patterns of singles varies by specific marital group. Widowed persons are the most involved group in church life. About half of all widowed persons attend church during a typical week. Never-married persons are the least likely group to regularly participate in religious activities: during a typical week, less than one-third of the never-married population attends church. In 1983 the percentage of never marrieds attending weekly was 29 percent, down from 31 percent in 1975. Divorced and separated persons have shown a recent downward trend in church participation rates: only 30 percent attended weekly in 1983, down from 40 percent in 1975.[9]

In the 1984 Gallup report, religion was rated as very important or fairly important by 91 percent of widowed persons, 88 percent of married persons, 84 percent of divorced persons, and 78 percent of never-married persons.[10] Even though church participation rates are low for never marrieds and divorced/separated persons, singles still place significant value on the importance of religion.

Singles in the Future

Will the single population continue to grow as a significant force in American society? Can recent trends be used to project the impact of singles in 1990? These questions are vital as churches plan to reach people with the good news of Jesus Christ. The changing age structure of the population offers insights into the role of singles in the future.

By 1990 the population aged eighteen to twenty-four will have declined as the end of the baby boom passes out of this age group. Because males tend to marry younger females and because the number of young women will decline, the percentage of young, never-married men will likely continue to increase. The percentage of young, never-married women is projected to remain the same; on the one hand, young women will face pressures to marry, but on the other hand, their rising education levels and career aspirations may lead them to continue to delay marriage. The never marrieds in older age groups will increase slightly as some of the large group of currently young, never marrieds choose to remain single.

The proportion of the population widowed is expected to remain at current levels due to "a slowdown in the divergence of male and female mortality rates over the age of 55."[11] However, older adults will be the second fastest growing age group in the 1980s, so the actual number of widowed persons may increase significantly.

Perhaps the fastest growing of all marital groups in the 1980s will be divorced and separated persons. The main contributor to this projection is not a rising divorce rate but, again, the aging of the baby boom population. From 1981 to 1983 the number of divorces in the United States dropped for the first time since 1962; however, as the size of the population aged twenty-five to fifty-four grows in the next decade, there is a potential for the number of divorces to rise even if the divorce rate goes down.

Actual projections for specific populations are subject to a great margin of error. Nevertheless, based on the assumptions above, the 1990 adult United States population is projected to be comprised of 72.5 million singles (up 8.0 million or 12 percent from 1983) and 112.8 million marrieds (up 10.3 million or 10 percent). The projected increase for singles can be subdivided for each category of singles. Never-married persons will number 38.6 million, up only 8 percent over 1983 after an increase of 50 percent from 1974 to 1983. Widowed persons are projected to number 14.7 million, up 1.9 million or 14 percent over 1983; and, finally, divorced/separated persons will number 19.2 million, up 3.4 million or 22 percent.[12]

Implications for Churches

1. The term *singles* refers not only to persons who have never married but also to persons who are divorced, separated, or widowed. As a total group, singles will continue to form a significant proportion of the population. Of every ten adults, four are single and six are married. This ratio of singles to marrieds is not expected to change in the 1980s although growth rates will differ for the three categories of singles. With a projected count of 72.5 million single persons in 1990, singles are a population segment that churches should actively seek to reach.

2. In planning ministries, churches should consider the specific profiles of singles. In 1983, 84 percent of never marrieds were eighteen to thirty-four years old, 74 percent of divorced/sepa-

31

rated persons were twenty-five to fifty-four years old, and 89 percent of widowed persons were fifty-five years old or over. Never-married males outnumbered never-married females 19.9 million to 16.0 million; divorced/separated females outnumbered divorced/separated males 9.6 million to 6.2 million; widowed females outnumbered widowed males 10.9 million to 1.9 million.[13]

3. For most persons, singleness is a transitory stage of life. Most never marrieds will eventually marry; by 1990 it is projected that only 6 percent of the population thirty-five years old or over will have never married. Most divorced persons will remarry and even widowed persons seek new marriages. Churches can minister to the needs of these persons in their current state and provide counsel through periods of life transition.

4. During the past decade, young adult singles have been the fastest growing group in Sunday School in Southern Baptist churches. From 1976 to 1983 their Sunday School enrollment increased 37 percent.[14] Because of the sheer size of the young singles population, many churches have been able to establish singles departments with minimum effort. Between 1983 and 1990, the population eighteen to thirty years old will begin to decline, but they will still represent the largest group of all single adults. In the coming years, churches may have to plan more aggressively to reach this special population group.

5. Churches need to examine the role of singles in the church. Although more singles are attending church, the national weekly church participation rates of never-marrieds and divorced/separated persons are well below rates for marrieds and widowed persons. These lower participation rates reflect a lowered value placed on the importance of religion, but they may also indicate churches are not meeting the needs and interests of singles. The aging of the baby boom will likely be accompanied by a renewed interest in religion, and churches should be prepared to address that interest.

6. Even though the divorce rate declined from 1981 to 1983, divorced/separated persons are projected to be the fastest growing marital category to 1990. Churches should plan to offer special care and concern for persons who have experienced broken marriage relationships. At the same time, churches can promote

a healthy view of marriage expectations and build support systems to lessen the likelihood of divorce or separation for currently married persons.

7. Churches in metropolitan settings will have a greater opportunity to reach never-married and divorced/separated persons. Three-fourths of these two groups of singles live in cities, while only two-thirds of marrieds and widowed persons are in metropolitan areas.

8. Only about one-half of all singles live with other family members, while one-third live alone and one-sixth live with nonfamily members.[15] Singles living alone have been the fastest growing household type since 1980. The nuclear family has traditionally been a source of meaningful life; however, with more persons living outside the nuclear family, the church has the potential for providing the community and relationships necessary for meaningful existence.

-----

1. U.S. Bureau of the Census, Current Population Reports, Series P-20, no. 389, *Marital Status and Living Arrangements: March 1983* (Washington, D.C.: U.S. Government Printing Office, 1984), table 1, p. 8, and U.S. Bureau of the Census, Current Population Reports, series P-20, no. 271, *Marital Status and Living Arrangements: March 1974* (Washington, D.C.: U.S. Government Printing Office, 1974), table 1, p. 13.

2. Ibid., first reference.

3. Ibid., both references.

4. U.S. Bureau of the Census, *Historical Statistics of the United States, Colonial Times to 1970,* part 1 (Washington, D.C.: U.S. Government Printing Office, 1975), p. 49.

5. Arland Thornton and Deborah Freedman, "The Changing American Family," *Population Bulletin,* vol. 38, no. 4 (Washington, D.C.: Population Reference Bureau, 1983), p. 6.

6. U.S. Bureau of the Census, Current Population Reports, series P-20, no. 349, *Marital Status and Living Arrangements: March 1979* (Washington, D.C.: U.S. Government Printing Office, 1979), table 1, p. 7.

7. Thornton and Freedman, pp. 8-9.

8. See note 1.

9. The Gallup Report, *Religion in America 1984* (Princeton: Princeton Religion Research Center, 1984), p. 57, and the Gallup Opinion Index *Religion in America 1976* Princeton: The American Institute of Public Opinion, 1976), p. 27.

10. The Gallup Report, *Religion in America 1984,* p. 34.

11. George Masnick and Mary Jo Bane, *The Nation's Families: 1960-*

1990 (Cambridge, MA: Joint Center for Urban Studies of MIT and Harvard University, 1980), p. 37.

12. Research Division, Home Mission Board, unpublished data, 1984.

13. See note 1, first reference.

14. *The Quarterly Review,* vol. 44, no. 4 (Nashville: The Sunday School Board of the Southern Baptist Convention, 1984), p. 32, and vol. 38, no. 4, p. 32.

15. U.S. Bureau of the Census, Current Population Reports, series P-20, no. 389, *Marital Status and Living Arrangements: March 1983* (Washington, D.C.: U.S. Government Printing Office, 1984), table 6, pp. 36-37.

Part II
Groupings of Single Adults

5
Never Married, College Singles
MILT HUGHES

The mental image conjured up when one thinks of "college students" is as varied as life itself, depending on one's experience, age, background, and current contact with students. Some think of a bunch of rebels freeloading on the taxpayer with minimal tuition responsibility. Others feel threatened by those who are gaining an education and acquiring an expertise designed to displace them in the marketplace. Others visualize wild fraternity parties, sexual looseness, and irresponsibility. Some visualize kids just out of high school, away from home for the first time, facing adult situations, and learning to cope with the massive challenge of adult life.

College students come from a vast slice of American life. They represent all ages; most are commuters; many have full- or part-time jobs.

For our study, we will focus on a particular segment of the student population: unmarried, undergraduate, usually between eighteen to twenty-three years of age, living on or near the campus. While there is no such thing as a "typical student," some common characteristics seem to surface in most cases.

1. While there is a wide variety of unmarried undergraduates, and a vast difference in academic settings, students are generally very much alike in their needs and desires. When you strip away the outer shell of academia, they look the same. This was made

clear to me a few years ago when I led retreats and seminars back to back in Boston and on a remote, rural campus in a Southern state. The retreat with Harvard, Yale, and MIT students was challenging. They asked tough questions. They weren't satisfied with simple answers. They were thinkers. We discussed individual needs, intellectual challenges to the faith, the reliability and relevance of Scripture, and how to be a growing, effective Christian in the context of an Ivy League school. I left Boston with deep intellectual-spiritual stimulation. I flew immediately to what might be the most remote and tiny Baptist college in our Convention. Many of the students had barely made the minimum academic requirements to get in. They weren't very intellectual; they didn't phrase their questions in the same manner; but we discussed individual needs, practical challenges to the faith, the reliability and relevance of Scripture, and how to be a growing, effective Christian in a small campus community.

At first, the contrast stunned me. What a difference! Yet in two or three days on that small campus, I came to realize some very important truths. Underneath, they were the same. They had the same deep inner needs. They were really looking for the same things. I concluded that, beneath the surface, students are very much alike! (While I found this to be true, I fully realize that our approach to reaching students and seeking to meet their needs must be flexible and carefully designed to minister to a particular kind of campus.)

2. Students are involved in the search for truth and meaning to life. This is not an oversimplification. It is expressed in different ways and from varying perspectives on value, but it is taking place. Students want to build their lives on something that makes sense, something that is practical and workable. They are looking for security in employment, companions, marriage, and other relationships.

3. Students are in the process of making some crucial life decisions. Usually, by the time they graduate, they have dealt rather seriously with at least two of these biggies: marriage and career. More and more are postponing marriage, but they at least are thinking through the question of whether and who. They may change majors several times, but usually by graduation have a pretty good idea of where they are going careerwise. Most will

seriously consider graduate school to further their chances of success in a given field.

A third big decision may well depend on how effective we are in our ministry to the students: the decision related to faith. By the time they graduate, most students have pretty well decided whether or not it makes sense to believe in God.

4. Students are teachable, flexible, and adventurous. The very fact that they enroll in college causes them to be open to new ideas and information. They are not set in cement. They can change. They are not afraid to try new ways of doing things.

As we take a look at unmarried college students, we can conclude several things:

All students need Jesus Christ in their lives.

They can be led to see this need because of their sensitivity to truth, relevance, and change.

These needs can be met with creative, relevant approaches, adapted for each unique situation.

They remain our most vital, untapped area of ministry and evangelism.

Students as a Resource

The characteristics listed above are true also of Christian students. In addition, however, they have taken the crucial step of committing their lives to Jesus Christ. They are in process of synthesizing truth and making it subservient to the lordship of Christ. They are finding meaning, purpose, and security in Jesus. They are teachable, flexible, and adventurous for Him. What a rich reservoir of potential for spiritual revival!

Their location on campus places them as "insiders" in the midst of a vast, largely unreached segment of society. They touch professors, TA's, administrators, athletes, internationals, dormies, and other varieties of fellow students. They are the best (and sometimes the only) resource for reaching the campus.

Let's take a look at a typical Baptist student as a resource.

1. Students active in Baptist Student Union (BSU) are involved and trained in a balance between the journey inward and the journey outward. They spend a lot of time developing their inner resources through Bible study groups, individual quiet times,

and discipleship training. This inner development equips them for an effective journey outward.

2. Students active in BSU are likely to be highly involved in missions and evangelism. The central thrust of the BSU philosophy and objectives tilts them in this direction. They study missions; they raise financial support for fellow students or go themselves as summer missionaries; they use prayer calendars for undergirding missions; they receive training in witnessing; they are involved in some kind of evangelistic emphasis-outreach during the year. The ratio of new converts to church members is about 1:38. In BSU it is 1:21.

3. Students active in BSU are more likely to be involved in leadership in their local church. I am constantly amazed at how many eighteen- to twenty-three-year-olds are teaching Sunday School, playing piano, directing music, heading up mission organizations, serving on committees, serving as youth directors, staffing Vacation Bible Schools and Backyard Bible Clubs. At weekend state BSU meetings (conventions and leadership training conferences), there is usually a 20 to 40 percent drop in attendance on Sunday morning. Why? Not because of waning interest or laziness, but because they are preaching, teaching, or leading in a local church somewhere.

4. Students active in BSU are developing innovative skills in communicating the gospel. They are learning and using drama, mime, clowning, contemporary music, puppets, dialogue, creative writing, competitive sports, marathons, homecoming parades, and many other approaches. They know that if they are to gain a hearing among a possibly hostile and hardened audience, they must outthink their contemporaries.

Many students, while not active in BSU, have achieved some of the same results through training received in their local churches.

Students can become a valuable resource in leading out in revival and renewal. In the mid-1940s a phenomenal movement gained national recognition: the student-led youth revival movement. Coming largely out of Texas BSUs, it rapidly spread to all parts of the traditional SBC areas. A major influence in my own ministry was a 1949 campus revival led by one of the Texas college students, Jess Moody. The movement is still with us today as BSU students conducted 2,141 revivals in churches in 1983-84.

Since the late 1940s, the national office of Southern Baptist student ministry has been instrumental in involving students in mission projects through the Home Mission Board, Foreign Mission Board, and state conventions. Tens of thousands of students have given up many summers to serve in needy mission areas. Many SBC leaders today once served as summer missionaries. Dr. Lloyd Elder, president of the Baptist Sunday School Board, was led to Christ through a summer missionary in Alaska.

When you begin to develop a strategy for revival and evangelistic outreach, don't forget your students. The tendency is to look to other adults, stable families, deacons, experienced leaders, to the neglect of the less mature, inexperienced, often undependable student. The church will be richer for utilizing unmarried students in key places of outreach leadership. They will bring fresh enthusiasm, creative ideas, lots of experience, uninhibited involvement, and a spirit of youth to the body of Christ and its desire for revival.

Students as Recipients

Elton Trueblood said, "When the church is looking for a mission field, it need not look past its nearest campus."[1] Two decades of the changing campus scene have not altered the validity of this statement.

Several factors seem to indicate that unmarried students are a key target area for evangelism.

1. They are searching for a meaning in life and for truth. This has been stated in the chapter introduction. If we have the truth in Jesus, we can offer a valid answer for their search.

Engraved on the administrative tower at the University of Texas, Austin, is the biblical verse "You shall know the truth, and the truth shall make you free."

A bold statement, engraved in marble on a building of a leading secular institution of higher learning.

2. They need an option. Their available data from which to determine faith and discover meaning is severely limited without information concerning Jesus. I was talking with a hotel clerk at Princeton, New Jersey. Jeff was a philosophy major at Rutgers

University. I asked if he had discovered a philosophy that really made sense to him, one to which he was willing to commit his life. He expressed confusion and indecision in his search. I asked him if he had ever studied the philosophy of Jesus, to which he said no. I challenged him to check out Jesus as recorded by the apostle John. Jeff was trying to make a crucial life decision without adequate information. He needed an option.

We need to see evangelism among the students as offering them an alternative to what they have discovered so far.

3. They need a clear explanation of the gospel. Many students in the USA have never had anyone share with them what it means to know Jesus Christ. Julie was such a person. I met her on a flight over Virginia. Our conversation led to a discussion of what it really meant to be a Christian. I asked her, "Has anyone ever sat down with you and explained to you how to become a Christian?" The answer was no. Although she was a graduate of a large university in Richmond, Virginia, no one had ever shared with her. Multitudes of students have been to church, listened to preachers, and wondered about the whole confusing issue of faith, but have never had anyone share personally with them.

4. They will be the future shapers and leaders of American life. If we influence them as students, they will become spiritual leaders of many nations. When you reach a student, you usually reach a leader.

5. International students will be shapers of world politics and industry. At one point, 75 percent of the presidents and prime ministers of the nations of the world had been students in the United States. Many of these are from countries where missionaries are not permitted. Recently, a student from Mainland China was led to Christ through the Baptist Student Union on a northern campus. The students there intend to disciple her as thoroughly as possible during her years as a student. She will be returning to China with more clout than a Caucasian American missionary could ever wield!

Some suggestions for seeing students as recipients.

1. When planning in-church evangelistic emphases, think creatively and use approaches which will attract students to the simplicity and awesomeness of Jesus, not insulting their intelligence

by manipulative methods. Use students to reach students: testimonies, drama, contemporary music, mime, puppetry, etc.

2. When doing evangelism on the campus, work with and through the Baptist Student Union. They are the officially recognized group on campus. They have an inside track the local church does not usually have. They know the "rules" within which to operate in doing outreach.

3. Realize that well-trained Christian students can be your greatest asset in penetrating the barriers of campus life. They are already on the inside. They already know the territory. Learn to use them effectively and help equip them for campus outreach. They know how to talk the language of the campus.

4. Concentrate on long-term relational evangelism. Short-term revivals may reach some students, but most will be reached through the individual touch: building relationships, establishing credibility, earning the right to be heard, meeting needs, and sharing the gospel with love and a serving heart. Crusade-type evangelism tends to turn off more students than it turns on.

Elton Trueblood's statement still stands. Your greatest mission field may very well be the nearest campus to your church. Utilize your students in planning and conducting effective evangelistic outreach on that campus.

---

1. Elton Trueblood, *The Company of the Committed* (New York: Harper and Brother, 1961), p. 12.

6

Never Married, Career Singles

DONNA CHRISTIAN MCCONNICO

Never married, career single is a classification that includes those who have chosen to remain single and those who have not yet had the opportunity to marry. Consider Scott, an attractive, well-educated, single adult who has never married. He is a white-collar worker with an upwardly mobile career. He has friends through the professional organization to which he belongs and the sports club where he works out. He's got it made—a great job, new car, nice apartment, friends! His question to me was, "Why do I need Christ and the church?" This chapter will address Scott's question and develop a strategy for evangelism to the never married, career single.

Several obstacles must be overcome in order to reach these singles for Christ. The first is the church's perception of never married, career singles. We have been guilty of viewing singleness as a temporary state, as if singleness is an undesirable condition. We must begin to perceive singleness as desirable, and we must teach our singles to view themselves as whole people.

Another message the church has conveyed is that "marriage is associated with maturity and singleness with immaturity."[1] Singles who are well educated and have demanding and responsible jobs will not respond to a church that views them as irresponsible or immature. The church must demonstrate a positive attitude by making never married, career singles a significant part of leadership structure. Singles must be actively pursued to serve as deacons, to teach, and to serve on meaningful committees.

Another hurdle that must be jumped is singles' perceptions of the church. Many never married, career singles view the church with apathy. They agree with Scott that the church does not seem to offer them anything. Some see it as a crutch for those who cannot handle life. Others see it as a naive, unintelligent, and restrictive choice. Mainline churches have been pictured in a legalistic light offering judgmental attitudes to those with different life-styles. The church must respond in love and relevance. We must offer programming that meets the needs of never married, career singles.

Where do we begin in mobilizing never married, career singles for evangelism? The easiest place to begin is Sunday School. Never married, career singles are often well educated and ambitious in their pursuit of career goals. They have a level of sophistication that breeds high expectations. Sunday School must gain the reputation for well-planned, creative teaching when relating to the career single. Sunday School yields three groups for evangelism: Sunday School members, Sunday School visitors, and friends of Sunday School members. A comparison of Sunday

School membership and church membership would yield many prospects for evangelism; a surprising number of members have no relationship with Christ. Those who visit our churches are usually receptive to Christ. Our Sunday School and worship service visitors need immediate follow-up from our singles. We must reach them while they are interested. Another target group is friends of Sunday School members. Our never married, career singles are the best tool we have for reaching never married, career singles. Our members should feel challenged to verbalize their relationship with Christ to their friends. They should also feel challenged to bring their friends to Sunday School.

In addition to Sunday School, singles can be reached through other programming. We must look at the needs of never married, career singles to see what they will respond to. A recent survey among singles at Dawson Memorial Baptist Church in Birmingham, Alabama, revealed that the top five needs never married singles under 35 perceived in themselves were Bible study, fellowship, prayer, financial planning and budgeting, and preparation for marriage. Unchurched singles may be responsive to opportunities for recreation such as aerobics or softball teams. Creative social planning may draw some singles. This group is generally very fitness conscious, so physical activity will appeal to them. Courses on sexuality and preparation for marriage will also interest career singles. Once singles have had a positive contact with our churches and our singles, they will be more responsive to a witness.

Never married, career singles are an excellent resource for evangelism. They have excellent capabilities in communication, so verbalization of the gospel should be less difficult for them than it is for other groups. Career singles are in the habit of acquiring knowledge, and they assimilate information very quickly. This enables them to learn methods of evangelism quickly. *EvangeLife*[2] and *Continuous Witness Training*[3] are two excellent programs of evangelism training. Perhaps a testimony workshop would help singles formulate a verbal witness. Preparation for evangelism will enable singles to feel more confident when they tell others about Christ. Our goal should always be a life-style of informal evangelism: singles sharing Christ with roommates, co-workers, family and friends; confronting others with Christ

43

through our words and our actions. How do we motivate our career singles to evangelize? We must preach the need for Christ in our pulpits, teach it in our classes, pray for a renewed desire to share, and offer opportunities to improve our verbal witness.

Let us return to Scott's question, "Why do I need Christ and the church?" First, without Christ, Scott will spend eternity separated from God. Scott will miss the most wonderful relationship that man can have. Christ died to pay for Scott's sin so that Scott can be in fellowship with God. Another reason that Scott needs Christ is because Christ gives meaning to life. Christ gives security in a faith that transcends the temporal. Scott needs the church because it serves Christ. The common cause of Christ unites us with others in a unique relationship. How do we get Scott and others like him to recognize their need for Christ?

"We must create within the lost a demand for the spiritual. . . . We are to do something for them and with them that will create within them such a demand for the spiritual that they will be compelled to come to church because they cannot stay away."[4] A personal strategy for reaching the lost begins with prayer. Prayer creates in us a desire to see others come to Christ. Communication with God also helps us to be more sensitive to His leading. The second element in reaching the lost is a victorious life-style. Others will respond to Christ when they see Him evident in our lives because of the genuine concern for others that we have. John 13:35 says, "By this shall all men will know that you are My disciples, if you have love for one another." The third important element in reaching the lost is the verbal witness. We are compelled to tell others the greatness of Christ's love for us. The last ingredient in personal evangelism is follow-up. We must continue to care for the people we share with so that they will experience a great desire to know Christ.

Reaching never married, career singles for Christ requires a strategy for drawing them to our churches and a strategy for sending a witness to them. We must develop formal and informal witnesses among our career singles. We must utilize the valuable resources we have in never-married singles. They have much to offer in service, talent, and energy. John 4:35 says, "Lift up your eyes, and look on the fields, that they are white for harvest." Never married, career singles are ready for the harvest.

44

1. Dr. Ferris Jordan, "Singles: The New Expression in Contemporary Society," sermon presented at the First Single Adult Ministers' Conference, Nashville, 1984.

2. Dan Crawford, *EvangeLife: A Seminar in Lifestyle Evangelism* (Atlanta: Home Mission Board, 1982).

3. *Continuous Witness Training* (Atlanta: Home Mission Board, 1982).

4. Roy J. Fish and J. E. Conant, *Every Member Evangelism for Today* (New York: Harper and Row, 1982), p. 58.

7

Divorced Singles

WOODY NORTHCUTT

There are two categories of people in a divorce regardless of whether they are Christian: those who leave a marriage and those who are left. The leavers will have varying degrees of guilt with which to deal. Those left will definitely have to deal with rejection. Being a Christian does not absolve either of these emotions. They are real! They punish. They damage. Each day for the first few months is punctuated with "Oh God, how am I going to make it?" Survival is the first priority. Survival of self. Survival for the family's sake if children are involved. Survival of faith if Christ has been a part of that life. Survival! Some don't make it. The majority do.

Out of desperation the divorced person turns to various people and things to help forget, survive, cope, and rebuild.

The family of God's response to the divorced single has been varied. Some seem to openly accept the divorced single with warmth; some respond with reluctance. Others respond as the pastor who, when talking with a young divorced woman, said, "I think you would find better fellowship with those people. Our church is not equipped to deal with people in your situation."

And there are a few who openly refuse to respond, accept, or deal with the divorced single. When these fields are white for harvest (John 4:35) and Jesus says, "I sent you to reap that for

45

which you have not labored; others have labored" (v. 38), the church of Jesus Christ could be experiencing the greatest revival of the twentieth century.

Why aren't we? There is an attitude adjustment that must take place toward the divorced single before it will happen. I've seen it, and so have you—we have all been guilty.

A divorced person comes for church membership. We welcome her. When she wants to work or speak or help, we say, "Our church policy with regard to divorced people working is. . . ."

What does our church policy say about murderers, deceivers, liars, gossipers, etc.? Until we have adjusted our attitude, any effort to reach more divorced singles will be ineffective. Sin is sin! Jesus did not prioritize sin. He did not skirt around it. He did not categorize or computerize it. "Repent" is what He said about it. "Seek the kingdom of God first" is how He said to deal with it. Acknowledge it, confess it, repent from it, turn toward God in Christ Jesus, and cast all upon God's mercy—whether it be murder, drugs, gossip, lying, anger, or divorce—cast all upon God's loving grace.

Until the church adjusts its attitude in line with Jesus, the multitude of divorced singles will remain wandering in the wilderness of despair. Redemption is also recovering those lost in the darkness of divorce.

Some think (and would lead others to believe) that to accept divorced singles into the church family and allow them to use their God-given gifts to further the work of the church would be to condone divorce. If we follow that line of logic, then who is able to carry on the work in the church with Jesus? Can liars? Do we condone these actions or attitudes? What about gossipers? Who's to say thieves or deceivers can? Paul wrote, "There is none righteous, not even one" (Rom. 3:10). He continued: "But God demonstrates His own love toward us, in that while we were yet sinners, Christ died for us. Much more then, having now been justified by His blood, we shall be saved from the wrath of God through Him" (Rom. 5:8-9). We say God's saving grace forgives our lying lips, our deceiving hearts, our drug abuse—when we confess the sin in Jesus' name. It also works the same way for divorced singles. They have prayed, "Lord, forgive me—HELP

46

ME! Oh, God, deliver me!'" many times in their fight for survival. They do not need to do more than to acknowledge sin, confess, repent, turn to God, and throw themselves on the grace of God in Christ. Now they should be accepted, welcomed, and affirmed in the family of God. When the church has made this attitude adjustment or begins to move in this direction, then it can reach out honestly, lovingly to help the divorced single.

Who are the divorced singles? Some are not believers in the God of the Christian faith. Many are believers. All of them walk for a time in the dark, exhausted, angry, hurt, and fearful.

They are people with questions. Why? Why me, Lord? Why now? What went wrong? How could this thing happen to me? Is there any help at all for me? Is there any hope? How can I face my friends? My family? My church? How can I go on? Will God, can God, forgive me?

How do they feel? One said, "Divorce devastated me!" Another commented, "I was crushed." Still another: "I wanted to die, it hurt so bad."

They feel ashamed, embarrassed, angry, hurt, disappointed, guilty, and rejected. Most feel like failures. Many feel like second-class citizens. Some feel used. All feel hurt and fearful to some degree. Many feel lost in the sense of no direction in life or purpose anymore.

All are in need of a Savior. All need the warmth of Christ's arm around them. All need to hear Jesus say, "Come to Me, *all* who are weary and heavy-laden and I will give you rest. Take My yoke upon you, and learn from Me, for I am gentle and humble in heart; and you shall find rest for your souls. For my Yoke is easy and my load is Light" (Matt. 11:28, author's italics).

All need acceptance as to who and where they are. All need someone who really does care about them and their situation. All need a family or support system that is nonjudgmental. All need the grace of God in their lives to give them strength, hope, and courage to go on. They need to believe in a God who can still fulfill His purpose in them (Rom. 8:28; Jer. 29:11-13).

The nonbeliever in Jesus Christ needs a positive, loving witness of Jesus' saving power. He is already in the dark. He is trying to cope with rejection and anger alone. Depression and guilt weigh heavily upon him. He needs to know there is a God who

47

is an expert at dealing with anger, guilt, rejection, and forgiveness.

Most nonbelievers who are divorced are afraid of the church. They see the church as judgmental and condemning. Whether this is a projection of their own feelings is not important. What is important is that we, the church, pull down that barrier by reaching out with open hands and heart. We need to emphasize there is forgiveness for failure and power available to rebuild. We need to show them hope through this valley of despair. We can be the support system who will love them into the family of God by way of the cross.

Emphasis on the atonement for modern man will help reach the nonbelieving divorced single. An emphasis that teaches Jesus' death defeats the power of guilt and shame in life. An emphasis that Jesus' blood covers the past now and for eternity. An emphasis that there is victory over life's circumstances through the cross of Christ. And an emphasis that Jesus as burden bearer calls us to bear His burden for a lost, dying world—even divorced singles.

The believing, divorced single also fears the church sometimes because of a judgmental attitude. They fear condemnation and rejection from many within the church. One divorced person had this said to him: "I didn't expect to see you here today. How can you face these people?" For this reason, many Christians who are divorced shy away from the church for a while. They drop out of sight. They conveniently find themselves out of town on Sunday. They withdraw from people, especially the church. They are afraid. They are ashamed. They are humiliated.

To reach them, we must want to reach them. We must plan to reach them. We must pray to reach them. We must go out and get them.

They need to hear and believe that God's forgiveness reaches into the depths, even to Christian divorced people. They need to hear it from pastors, deacons, teachers, and members of the body of Christ. They need to be welcomed sincerely and nonjudgmentally. They need to be incorporated into the family of God as full citizens of the Kingdom.

They can serve on committees, work in Sunday School, lead seminars, give testimonies, and work with boys, girls, and youth.

They can help put together seminars and conferences for singles in the community with the church's help. They can speak to young marrieds about the pitfalls to be aware of in marriage. At the pastor's request, they can talk with couples contemplating marriage. They can grow into strong, dynamic witnesses for Jesus —if given a helping hand, an opportunity and responsibility.

A church can begin by surveying the community or its own church membership for divorced singles. A meeting can be called to discuss needs and feelings. From this, a class or a group can be formed.

Some churches have divorce recovery workshops for singles in their community. Many denominational agencies have resource material to help any church who genuinely wants to reach out to singles who are divorced and living in their community.

Do we really care? Is Jesus' statement the church's statement, "Come to me, *all* [of you]" (Matt. 11:28, author's italics)?

8

Separated Singles

GARY D. CHAPMAN

"I'm not single; I'm separated." Many may feel the way this individual does and wonder why a chapter on the separated should be included in a book on singles. Strictly speaking, separated persons are not single, but they are alone. They are no longer living with their spouses. Their dream of marital unity has turned into a nightmare, and they are now apart. Married but not together—single but not free—many separated individuals feel they no longer have a place in society. They cannot relate to their married friends in the same manner they did before, yet they may not feel comfortable with the singles group. They live in a social no-man's land.

Fortunately, separation is a temporary state. I like to picture it as a long hallway with a door at either end. One door is labeled "divorce" and the other "reconciliation." Separated persons with all their hurt, disappointment, anger, resentment, bitterness, loneliness, and ambivalent feelings may be lying in the hallway too weak to get up and walk through either door, but eventually they will walk or crawl through one of those doors. Separation is not forever!

Physical separation, when one partner actually moves out of the house or apartment, is a time of emotional trauma. The couple has likely had problems for some time. Conflict, frustration, and feelings of emptiness and emotional distance may have been around for a long time, but in the past the couple has stayed together. Now they are separated. "What will happen to me now? What will happen to . . . ? Is this it? Will we get back together? What if we don't? How about finances? What about the children? What about our parents? Oh, God, what have we done?" These and a thousand other questions flood the mind of the separated person.

Sometimes the couple has talked and mutually agreed that separation is what they want to do. More often, however, for any number of reasons, one spouse chooses to leave without the consent of the other. Sometimes a third party is involved. Sometimes physical or mental abuse has reached an intolerable level, and one chooses separation as an escape route. Sometimes conflict or apathy has taken its toll. Often after separation, one spouse really wants a chance to work on the marriage and the other has lost hope. For both, it is a time of emotional upheaval.

In this unsettled and frustrated state, many separated people turn to the church for help. While they are questioning life's meaning, they are in a unique position to take a fresh look at the spiritual dimension of life. Many have not been to church in years, but now they are open. The church must be ready not only to meet emotional needs but also to lead them to spiritual reality.

During this separated period, which may last from a few days to several years, the church has a unique opportunity to minister to its own and reach out to the unchurched and unsaved. After the initial expressions of sympathy, married friends often quietly withdraw from the separated person—not because they do not care but because they do not know what to say or do. The church's singles ministry is uniquely qualified to minister to the separated. Many of those in the singles ministry have experienced the pain of separation and are willing to invest the necessary time to listen, understand, and encourage the separated. Many of them also found Christ after their own separation and are now equipped to share Christ with others.

Some will object, feeling that a divorced Christian working with a separated individual would tend to encourage divorce rather than the biblical ideal of reconciliation. This has not been my observation. The divorced Christian is strongly motivated from his own experience to encourage reconciliation. He knows firsthand the pain and difficulty of divorce. Many of the divorced singles in our ministry have been used of God to lead separated persons to reconciliation to God and their spouses. Obviously, not all separated persons will be able to reconcile, for reconciliation requires the efforts of both members of the marriage. One cannot effect reconciliation alone. The church's singles ministry then becomes the support system to walk with the separated person through the trauma of divorce and the process of rebuilding life.

Ultimately, the most helpful thing we can do for non-Christians who are separated is to lead them to faith in Christ. When they find Christ, they gain not only forgiveness of sins and eternal life but instruction and power for daily living. They now have a point of reference (Christ and Scripture) around which they can begin to organize their lives. Life will take on new purpose and fulfillment, whatever happens to their marriage. As Christians, they are now a part of a family from which they gain emotional, spiritual, and social support. The church is a fellowship of forgiven sinners eager to receive others and grow toward Christlikeness.

Does that sound ideal? The following suggestions are given with the desire that the ideal may become reality in your church.

Strategies for Reaching the Separated for Christ

1. *Train single adults to evangelize.* We will never reach our potential in winning the separated to Christ until we have trained Christian singles to share Christ as a way of life. Use EvangeLife, Continuing Witness Training, or some other program, but make sure that your singles know how to lead someone to Christ.

2. *Create an evangelistic atmosphere.* I don't mean singing "Just As I Am" in the Sunday School class. I mean talking about the

priority of leading people to Christ. Let them see by your example that you believe that the greatest thing you do is share the gospel. Help them to think evangelism. Then as they have opportunity to minister to the separated, they will seek to minister to the whole person: emotional, physical, social, and spiritual. If we do not emphasize the spiritual, we are no more than a secular community support group. We are being unfair and unchristian to those to whom we minister.

3. *Provide counseling.* This may be the first point of contact separated persons will have with the church. Counseling in our society has gained not only acceptance but popularity. Thus, it is perfectly normal for separated persons to turn to the church for counseling. If no counselor is available, they will go elsewhere and the church has lost an opportunity.

In smaller churches, the pastor does most or all of the counseling. In larger churches there may be full-time professional Christian counselors on staff. In all of our churches, we have laypeople gifted of God with abilities for listening, understanding, and encouraging others. These people can be trained in biblical principles and counseling techniques. Some of these can specialize in working with those recently separated. Many singles have the potential for this ministry. Counselors must see evangelism as one of their objectives.

4. *Create support groups.* These groups usually meet weekly for the purpose of providing a caring atmosphere in which those recently separated can share their hurt and ask honest questions. The leaders of this group should include individuals who have experienced separation. A balance between those who have divorced and those who have been reconciled to their spouses would be ideal. Each meeting should include a time of prayer. Leaders should be trained in evangelism and, at an appropriate time, share Christ with group members. This may best be done individually.

5. *Utilize books.* Books have the advantage of being available to speak on a moment's notice twenty-four hours a day and willing to repeat everything as often as you like. Books can be used: (1) to train Christians in how to evangelize and minister to the separated and (2) to stimulate the separated individual to take constructive action. My own book, *Hope for the Separated,*[1] is unique

52

in that it is written directly to the separated individual, encouraging the exploration of realistic reconciliation. Each chapter gives "growth assignments"—specific actions which the separated person may take toward growth in self-understanding, developing the relationship with God and the estranged spouse. The response to this book has been very encouraging.

Each singles class would do well to develop its own lending library with books made easily accessible each week. This may be done in conjunction with the church library where such exists. Certain books and evangelistic booklets should be available for free distribution.

6. *Take initiative in contacting couples who separate.* Marital separation is not limited to non-Christians. All too often when a couple in the church separates, it will be weeks before anyone contacts them—again, not because we do not care but because we "do not want to invade their privacy" or we "do not know what to say or do." The couple is hurting, going through the deepest valley of their lives, and no one comes. Thus, they conclude the church does not care. If one of them died, we would flock to the house without invitation; but when they separate, we are deathly silent and stay away in droves. This must change if we are to minister to the separated.

Church staff and lay leaders must be challenged to reach out immediately to couples who separate. In a spirit of love and concern, we must let them know that all the resources of the church are available to them. If the church does not have anyone able to counsel them, we should help them locate such a person and, if necessary, give financial assistance. Not everyone will respond to such an offer, but some will; and many marriages can be saved. Sometimes only one partner will respond to the love and care of the church. In such a case, we should pray for the other partner and minister to the one who is responsive. Perhaps in time the other will also respond. If not, and he or she insists on divorce, then the church can nurture the responsive partner through the pain of divorce into a productive life as a single-again.

7. *Educate church members on what the church has available* to the separated couple. If counseling is available, then make sure that all adults know and are encouraged to share this information with

their non-Christian friends who separate. Our people are in the marketplace and are able to be the link between the separated person and the church. If free materials are provided by the church, then see that adults know what is available and how to get it. A book or booklet given by a church member to a separated person may be the beginning of hope. As one reconciled husband said of *Hope for the Separated,* "If more separated folks would read this book, there would be fewer divorces." Many have also found Christ through reading the same book. Our laypeople are our best evangelizers, but we must train them in how to use the resources available.

8. *Concentrate on prevention program.* How can we best minister to the thousands of married couples who are on the road to separation in the 1980s and 90s? I believe one way is to contact them early on the marital road and administer preventive medicine. Get them involved in Bible study, discipleship programs, and marriage enrichment activities which will help them grow together.

I have been extremely encouraged with the results of a thirteen-week discipleship program for married couples called *Building Relationships?* which we have used in our church for the past two years. It is designed to build the couple's relationship with God and each other by such activities as daily quiet time with God and daily sharing time with one's spouse, weekly Bible study, Scripture memory, daily acts of service to spouse, learning the emotional love language of one's spouse, and how to handle anger and conflict constructively. Programs like this offer the greatest hope for Christian marriages. In turn, a strong Christian marriage may be the greatest evangelistic tool the church has in attracting the attention of the non-Christian world in the last decade of the twentieth century. The world desperately wants lasting, meaningful marriages. The church has the answer. We must not fail our generation by keeping it hidden (Matt. 5:15-16).

---

1. Gary D. Chapman, *Hope for the Separated* (Chicago: Moody Press, 1982).

2. Gary D. Chapman, *Building Relationships: A Discipleship Program for Married Couples* (Winston-Salem: Marriage & Family Life Consultants, Inc., 1983).

9

Widowed Singles

DOROTHY JOHNSON SIZEMORE

The comment of Alice of the memorable *Alice in Wonderland* as she struggles to understand her upside down world, "I knew who I was this morning, but I seem to have changed," could be uttered by every individual who has struggled for meaning, purpose, and identity following the death of a spouse. "Who am I?" becomes the question. "I knew who I was when my spouse was alive—but now everything has changed; I am no longer a half of a couple; I no longer have a life partner; I no longer have someone who shares my dreams, goals, concerns—in fact, I'm not sure about any dreams or goals. I am changed—and I am alone!"

The search for identity becomes paramount as the days move into weeks, and weeks into months. Life must go on—but how?

And They Came

Friends, neighbors, pastor, deacons, family—these and more help the surviving spouse through those first days of numbing existence. Flowers, cards, food, and phone calls provide loving support to ease the pain and fill the empty hours. But the day arrives when the flowers are wilted, the last dish has been returned, friends and family no longer call or visit, and suddenly two questions surface with overwhelming urgency—"Who am I?" and "Where do I go from here?"

Well-meaning friends and family members often attempt to console and comfort in ways that actually hurt more than help, as the newly widowed struggles to cope with the unfamiliar daily demands. The often-repeated platitudes and sympathy clichés mean very little when the very structure of life lies in a shattered heap. "You must not cry; everything will be all right." "It was her time to die." "God knows best" or "You can make it" serve little purpose. The quiet support of a friend's presence means far more than a barrage of well-intended but meaningless words when one must deal with the depths of grief plus the newly defined daily responsibility of bills, job, children, car maintenance, plumbing, laundry, and a multitude of other stresses.

55

A Time to Grieve

The world of the widowed single adult is as varied as the hues of the midnight sun, with the diversity dependent upon multiple factors including age, education, experience, philosophy of life, religious orientation, and attitude. Several threads of commonality, however, weave a similar recognizable tapestry of existence as each struggles through predictable stages in the process of grief. These stages include shock, numbness, alternating between fantasy and reality, flooding of emotions and grief, selective memory and stabbing pain, and finally acceptance of loss and the reaffirmation of life.[1]

There is no strict timetable for grieving. The grieving process differs significantly with each individual in intensity and duration, with tremendous variation in the way people react. The shock of the loss of a spouse has been compared to radical surgery; a significant part of life has been severed, never to be regained.

The experience has been compared to walking alone through a long dark tunnel. Life continues to surround, but little awareness, interaction, or involvement occurs. The ever-present light at the end of the tunnel brightens and dims at irregular intervals as the bereaved struggles to move beyond the overwhelming sadness and fragmentation into a sense of wholeness once again.

Death of a mate, recognized by many leading psychologists as the single greatest human stress experience, thrusts the surviving spouse not only into the seemingly bottomless pit of grief, but demands an immediate reorganization and restructuring of the very core of existence. Questions never before faced now demand immediate answers; responsibilities heretofore shared must now be faced alone; unexpected emotions surface rendering one numb and incapable of action; and amidst the turmoil a cry of agonizing loneliness and despair pierces the heart: "My world has shattered, and I don't know where to begin in my struggle to once again find a meaningful, purposeful, satisfying existence."

The answers lie deep within each individual, but the search can be long and difficult and is never without pain. Personal attitude becomes of utmost importance.

A Time to Heal

Two pathways, and only two, emerge. One tumbles downward through grief into self-pity, futility, hopeless despair, and ultimate uselessness. The other struggles upward through grief, searching, hoping, reidentifying and reshaping into a significantly different life, but one solidly based upon a renewed self-identity, personal confidence, and an assurance of being fully human, fully alive. The power of personal choice rests with the individual and demands a daily reaffirmation of the chosen pathway.

The familiar cliché that "time is a great healer" has significant realistic application for those walking through grief. The passing of time does indeed make a difference. Gradually, ever so slowly, life begins to focus, new directions emerge, the possibility for new beginnings surface, and the dormant emotions of joy, happiness, and celebration begin to stir.

The widow/er is inevitably locked into change, and change can be exceedingly painful. Friendships change. "Old friends" often become uncomfortable in relationships with the new single adult and may casually back away from the usual encounters. Invitations may be extended less and less frequently ("I'm sure he'd feel uncomfortable being the only single," or "I'm afraid I'll say the wrong thing to her") which further isolates the widow/er and intensifies the feelings of aloneness. The continued support of old friends is essential, but of equal importance is the need to develop new friendships and new interests.

Life-styles change, habits change, personalities may change, and goals must change. A positive affirmation of this inevitable change is crucial to the successful emergency beyond the grief experience.

A personal commitment to "live one day at a time" allows the widow/er to concentrate on today's experiences of joy, struggle, accomplishment, change, or need. Yesterday's experiences must become treasured memories which free the individual to live today. No energy remains to meet the demands of today if all energy is focused toward the past.

The ability to accept what has happened, learn as much as possible from the experience, and then move beyond it into a new identity, a new direction, and a new focus, confident that

God has given to each of us the necessary inner strength to succeed, must become the goal of each widow/er in order to move beyond the grief experience into the fullness of life.

Sound of Celebration—Color of Joy

The journey from coping to acceptance to affirmation to celebration is indeed a lonely and tedious pilgrimage, but the pilgrim who chooses the upward pathway and accepts the challenge to grow through the pain of grief ultimately emerges not only changed but victorious.

The continual rediscovery that the God of Abraham, Isaac, and Jacob, the God of our fathers, the God of our youth, and the God of today is one and the same—and that His challenge to each of us is to live today to its fullest and to *BE* today all that He created us to be, whatever our marital status or life-style—demands that the widowed move beyond the darkness of grief into the light of creative celebration of life.

The church must play a significant role in this crucial transition through acceptance, support, affirmation, love, and challenge. The widowed single adult needs the church and the church needs the widowed single adult. Together they comprise the community of faith.

The widowed must be led to view life as a gift from God, a gift to be treasured whatever the duration. For beyond the questions without answers, the nameless fears, the endless nights, and the ceaseless tears rests the assurance that God's love surrounds, undergirds, and gives the strength and power to change the upside down world of grief into a world of faith, hope, and celebration.

---

1. Wayne E. Oates, *Anxiety in Christian Experience* (Waco: Word Books Inc., 1971).

10

Single Parents

J. CLARK HENSLEY

"For a number of years, the best evangelistic outreach group has been our Singles Again Class. Scarcely a week goes by but what someone from this group accepts Christ," stated the pastor of one of the largest churches in Jackson, Mississippi. The Sunday School teacher of the class recounted her experience on visitation night when five men who had never witnessed were the only ones to show. She loaded them in the church van and all six visited prospects together. The following Tuesday night the five novices, now with one week of experience, made fruitful contacts on their own. Similar testimonies are heard across the Southern Baptist Convention from churches who make a place for single parents in their ministry.

Nearly 13 percent of United States families were headed by single parents in 1982, according to the Census Bureau. They report that 45 percent of all children born today will spend at least one year living with one parent. It is estimated that 15,000,-000 children live in stepfamilies and perhaps another 4,000,000 live in and out of stepfamilies. These stepfamily children were for a time in single-parent homes.

Approximately one out of five children under eighteen in the United States now lives in a one-parent family. The term *one-parent* refers to a resident parent responsible for the care of the children. There may be a nonresident parent who shows some responsibility toward the children in support and some temporary care. Or the other parent may be deceased. It may be that the nonresident parent is irresponsible and indifferent toward the children.

Much diversity is found in one-parent families. But there are repeated patterns which give insight into the nature of most of them.

The vast majority of children live with their mother, but the number of fathers serving as the single parent is increasing. It is difficult for either a father or a mother to provide twenty-four-hour care and supervision of the children and still work at a full-time job. Many one-parent families are insecure. Most mothers from these families must work outside the home, and a large percentage do not have a high level of job training. Often the one-parent family has more children than the average family, with living conditions inadequate as to privacy, heating, or bathroom facilities.

Single Parents Are People, Too

The single parents and their children are people—flesh and blood, mind and spirit—with longings, loves, frustrations, and aspirations. Not only are they a considerable segment of the population, but most of them are making, or will make, a significant contribution to society.

The single parent often feels very much alone, even isolated. Church leaders need to recognize not only the numbers involved, but some of the challenges, tasks, and problems the single parent faces. Yet the single parent shares with other parents many common privileges and problems.

The Grief Process

It is difficult for some church leaders to understand that a divorce grief process is closely akin to the grief experience in terminal illness. In the initial phases, considerable confusion is experienced.

Finally, there is acceptance or the inner realization that this event is in the process of happening, or it has happened, and is final. The spouse has died or the marriage is dead. One thing is different in the case of the death of a marriage in that both persons are still alive to be a constant reminder of the past. This makes recovery more difficult. In the loss of a spouse by death, the minister and others of the church family support those in grief. In the loss by divorce, more often the grieving ones are ignored or "sides are chosen" to further complicate the church's being redemptive or a comforting support in the readjustment period.

The Unwed Parents

Unwed parents may have consciously chosen to have a child, but usually the births are unplanned. Most members of this group are teenagers and do not have the level of maturity required for effective parenting. Among other adjustment difficulties is the fact that the mother must drop out of school and becomes alienated from her peer group. She may become distrustful of others, while at the same time seeking to determine her identity. She has difficulty earning enough money to support herself and her child. Unfortunately, often her support systems (family, church, peer group) are very limited.

These observations usually do not apply to a single woman who may adopt a baby or young child. However, she will usually face the typical problems of single parenting.

Church Leaders' Understanding

Much has been written on single parenting. Our purpose here is to help church leaders better understand the needs and how the church may help minister to single parents. Church leaders and friends should understand where the single parent is in the grief process, then stand by—not necessarily with answers, but with presence and whatever practical help is needed. This may include child care, especially if a child should become ill and the parent must still go to work—or transportation for the children to attend church or community events. If special church activities are planned for single parents, thoughtful church leadership will provide for child care or activities suitable for the children. Church programs planned for parents should include single parents. Announcements and promotions should be handled so the single parent will feel included rather than excluded.

The church may help the single parent in the diffusion of dependencies. Before the loss of the spouse, there had developed a dependency on one other person to meet many needs. Now these dependencies need to be spread to significant others, such as banker, minister, lawyer, business adviser, parent, friend, service people, doctor, and others. But always, the parent needs to keep his/her identity and direction and not lean upon others in a self-destructive manner.

Cautions to Observe

A word of caution to church leadership. The gifts of single parents should be used in the program of the church and opportunities for using these gifts should be offered. In loneliness and the desire to be needed, one may easily be manipulated. The single parent has more than the usual demands upon energy and time, and he/she alone knows best how to use both. The single parent should be careful not to overtax his strength or neglect his family as a result of having guilt laid on him by someone, perhaps a pastor, who says, "Now this is the Lord's will for you" or "This is the Lord's work." Indeed, the caring pastor will help the single parents use their gifts to the best advantage while protecting some sharing time for family. This, too, is the Lord's work!

The thoughtful church leader will not label the single parent family as a "broken" family or "broken" home. A family may be interrupted by death, disrupted by divorce, or divided by separation, but is not "broken." Labels are misleading. It is better to identify a family by the family name and omit any label or descriptive adjective.

Help for the Children

Some church family members may assist the single parent in working on a maturing process through the adverse experience. Children adjust better when the resident parent behaves with maturity toward the event and the children. It is difficult to avoid being overprotective of children in their loss of a parent, and sometimes facts are distorted. Honesty is the best policy with appropriate consideration of the age and development of the children. Sometimes the pastor is in a position to be very helpful at this point.

Children of divorce often feel a loss of self-esteem. They may feel rejected, abandoned, unwanted, and unloved. Or they may feel responsible for the divorce and feel guilty about it. The church family should be sensitive to these feelings and be reassuring as to the worth of the persons involved. These children face the usual challenges of the stages of development and need encouragement. They are normal children in what they feel to be an abnormal situation. A genuine, caring church family is one of the greatest assets these children can have in developing a feeling of security.

Concern for the body of Christ demands concern in developing methods of meeting these needs. As parents must learn that unconditional love is the key to building and nourishing their family members, so should the church family offer such love and nourishment.

Church Programming

As the church evangelism ministry is developed, single parents must be included. The church should also include grandparents in programs of intergenerational guidance, and qualified single parents should be considered for leadership positions in the church.

Churches exist to build up persons in the mood of faith, hope, and love. Church members and leaders concerned about the dimensions of the soul of the church will, with a warm heart, extend a helping hand to the single parent. When this is done, single parents and their children will become both a field and a force for evangelism.

11

Singles with Alternative Life-Styles

BOB THRIFT

I recognized the voice on the phone because I had talked to her briefly the week before. She had said she wanted to come in to talk. Now she was calling from the campus hospital. I went by to visit and listen while she laid out before me a lifelong struggle which had led to a suicide attempt and her present hospitalization. What had brought this attractive, intelligent, Christian woman to the point of suicide?

He was referred to me by a close friend. He was thirty-two, single, active in his church, and a successful attorney. His depression was severe. He was hardly sleeping, had no appetite, and was struggling to keep his train of thought. What could bring this handsome, successful attorney to this point of severe depression?

Both of these individuals were suffering from a condition as old as the Scripture itself. They were gay. At least that is the term used today. Homosexual may be a better term, for many would say it is anything but gay.

Each of them had grown up within the church, but from their earliest memories had a stronger sexual urge for members of the same sex than for those of the opposite sex. Freudians would explain this as a fixation at an early psychosexual stage of development, while geneticists may talk of hormonal imbalance. And the theories go on. The purpose of this chapter is not to discuss the whys of this alternative life-style but to attempt to understand the need for a ministry to it. The important consideration is that a large segment of our society is homosexual, for whatever reason, and we as Christians have a responsibility to reach out to them.

There are studies, such as those done by Alfred Kinsey, which state that 1 to 3 percent of all females and over 16 percent of all males may be exclusively homosexual. By most accounts this is a conservative estimate. Because of these kinds of facts and the growing awareness of homosexuality, we as the church are going to have to respond to this too-long-ignored life-style.

One of the problems heterosexuals have in relating to homosexuality is that they cannot identify with it. If someone admits to being a thief, liar, adulterer, alcoholic, or embezzler, heterosexuals can understand how that is possible because they may have been tempted to act in one of these ways. But for heterosexuals, homosexuality becomes unimaginable. Telling someone who is homosexual to change sexual preference would be as difficult for them to accomplish as it would be for a heterosexual to change sexual preference. Because they cannot identify with it or may be afraid of their own homosexual tendencies, heterosexuals become intolerant and rejecting of those for whom homosexuality is a way of life.

Homophobia (irrational fear of homosexuality) has no place in the Christian church. Myths about homosexuality abound. Over 90 percent of the time child molesters are heterosexual, yet the myth continues of homosexuals luring innocent children into homosexual practices. To minister to the homosexual, we must first throw away the myths and stereotypes because there are no real stereotypes. Limp wrists and lisps are no more typical of homosexuals than ten gallon hats and six-shooters are typical of all Texans. The image of homosexuals lurking in the shadows waiting to snatch up our little boys is no more common than heterosexuals cruising our daughters in order to lead them into prostitution.

The young attorney I mentioned earlier shared with me his lifelong struggle agonizing over this "sinful" condition. He would spend hours praying for God to deliver him from it. Yet he continued to be as much a homosexual as others are heterosexual.

The young woman wrote me a letter several years later. She said she had finally accepted the fact that she was lesbian, but that God loved her anyway. She was living with another Christian lesbian and felt a joy and peace she had never before known in her Christian life. I saw her again about three years later, and she still felt the same way.

Over the years I have worked with many homosexuals; and though their backgrounds and experiences have been different, they have all felt unaccepted by the church and unable to turn to the church for help and support. I believe the issue of homosexuality and the church's response to it will be one of the most difficult issues the church will have to face for the rest of this century.

To do this, we must revise our vocabulary in order to change our attitude and approach to homosexuality. Just as the way we speak of blacks affects the way we relate to them, the way we speak of homosexuals affects the way we relate to them. Words such as *queer, fag, lesbo, fruit,* and *fairy* will have to be discarded just as *nigger, Sambo,* and *spade* had to be for the blacks.

We cannot minister to homosexuals until we are willing to see them as fellow human beings. When we can see them as also being "created in the image of God," then, and only then, can we minister to them in God's name. Nothing separates us from one another in the eyes of God. We are all His children. Once we accept that, then we can begin talking about providing a ministry to all people, including the homosexual.

A most important question to be asked is whether the emphasis in ministry to homosexuals is in changing their sexual preference or bringing them into a relationship with Jesus Christ. What about the homosexual as a Christian? Are the two terms compatible? Can one be both homosexual and Christian? No ministry to the homosexual can exist until this question is seriously dealt with.

The odds of a homosexual changing sexual preference are very slim. Masters and Johnson, as well as other sex researchers, acknowledge that seldom if ever can the homosexual change sexual orientation. Though there have been a few studies where, through intense aversion behavioral therapy, some have changed sexual behavior, no real long-term results have been documented to any extent. REGENERATION, a specialized ministry to homosexuals in Baltimore, has helped homosexuals to no longer continue in homosexual activity. However, it is uncertain to what degree their basic homosexual drive has been altered.

If the criterion for ministering to homosexuals is whether they can become heterosexual, then there may not be any chance for ministry. But nowhere did Jesus say, "Come unto me all ye who are straight." Instead he said, "Come unto me all ye who are heavy laden, and I will give you rest" (Matt. 11:28, KJV). Was He excluding anyone? Did He say, My grace is for everyone unless you are gay? Nothing keeps us from the availability of God's love and mercy.

If the church can work through its own homophobia and bring itself to the point of accepting the homosexual as equally worthy of God's salvation, then ministry may occur. But this acceptance is only the beginning point. The question now is, "Where do we go from here?"

James B. Nelson, a professor of Christian ethics, believes there are four basic positions the church may assume toward homosexuality. The first is "rejecting and punitive," which says the homosexual is rejected for his behavior and should be punished for it. Second is "rejecting and nonpunitive," which condemns the condition and acts of homosexuality without condemning the homosexual. Next is "conditional acceptance," which strives to accept homosexuals but nonetheless views them as inferior. The fourth and final position is "unconditional acceptance," which says they are different, nothing else.

We must struggle with which of these is most Christlike. Can we as followers of Christ accept any position which interprets whether a person is worth receiving God's love according to his

66

or her specific human behavior? Thank goodness God's love and grace toward me is not dependent upon my behavior. Did Christ ever qualify the availability of His love? The only qualifier was a willingness to follow after Him.

If the church is to take seriously this ministry, then it must also be willing to face the potential threat to the peace within the church. Can the church handle the possible conflict of an openly gay or lesbian couple applying for church membership? Sooner or later these issues will have to be faced by every church seeking to minister to singles, for a ministry to singles opens the door for a potential ministry to homosexuals.

The phrase "ministry to homosexuals" may be inappropriate. This connotes a specialized program similar to our youth programs or our ministries to the elderly. This is probably not the best approach. Unless the church has a special need for martyrdom or notoriety, no specialized ministry is warranted. The "gay Sunday School" or "lesbian night out" seems out of place.

Possibly the most appropriate approach is to help the church to develop a growing sensitivity to the issue of homosexuality and then be willing to meet their individual needs as you would any other church member's. To develop this sensitivity, the church may need to start with a discussion group on homosexuality from a Christian perspective. However this sensitivity is developed, it is important that the church begin now to face this pressing issue.

How aggressively the church wants to minister to this population will determine the approach chosen. Many singles already know homosexuals but have been afraid to witness to them for fear of the response of their church. With encouragement, these singles can begin reaching out to their homosexual friends and acquaintances.

How do we interpret scriptural passages, particularly out of the Old Testament, which speak to homosexuality? What kind of influence will the acceptance of homosexuals in the church have on the developing morals of our youth? These questions and others like them are going to have to be discussed within a framework of Christian compassion in order to witness and evangelize these fellow brothers and sisters in Christ.

To assist in this goal, I have listed some books which may prove helpful in confronting these issues. I pray that God will be a part of all our churches in this difficult but important ministry.

_____

Drakeford, John. *A Christian View of Homosexuality.* Broadman Press, 1977.
Field, David. *The Homosexual Way: A Christian Option?* Inter-Varsity Press, 1979.
Nelson, James. *Embodiment.* Augsburg Press, 1979.
Scanzoni, Letha and Molenkott, Virginia Ramey. *Is the Homosexual My Neighbor? Another Christian View.* Harper and Row, 1978.
Switzer, David K. and Shirley. *Parents of the Homosexual.* The Westminster Press, 1980.

12

Handicapped Singles

RANDY GALLAWAY

Handicapped single adults have the same hopes, feelings, fears, guilts, doubts, and needs as any other persons in our society. The main difference with someone who is handicapped is in the area of felt needs. More than any other persons in our society, handicapped people desire acceptance. For many, childhood was a very painful experience. If they were born with disability, they often endured the teasing and ridicule of other children. Later in life, they experienced the fact that many adults tend to shy away or ignore any person with a disability. When we as Christians reach out to make a friendship with a handicapped person, it's a special event in that handicapped person's life.

Our outreach, in the name of Christ, needs to begin with accepting the person as he is. It may require taking time to learn about the individual's disability. How did he become disabled? Has he been disabled since birth? Was the handicap due to a sickness or accident? At what point did he become handicapped, and how did he feel about this? Some blame God for their physical situation, and this becomes a serious barrier to genuine faith and trust in Christ.

Dignity is another area of need of a handicapped person. Many feel they have lost their dignity due to years in the hospital or in rehabilitation. They feel as if they have no private, personal rights. They may be dependent upon others and may be forced to live in total dependence upon family, caretaker, or a group-care system. When we treat them as confident, whole persons who have a physical limitation but are of value and dignity before God, we raise their self-esteem. In doing this, we open the door for the gospel. Human value is not in the outward things you can do, such as physical strength or athletic ability, but the image of God in us. It is our personality, our spiritual capacity, and our moral character that counts. In these areas Christ can make a physically distorted person whole again, and this is part of our message.

Personhood is another element of this same dilemma. How can I be a person in spite of limitations on my abilities? We say, as Christians, that God sees you as a person, and we see you as a person. We want to know you and have fellowship with you as a person, not as a victim or a casualty of life. We see you as a person, made in the image of God. You have a destiny to fulfill.

Genuine friendship is the key that opens the door to handicapped people. Time invested in building a friendship with a handicapped person returns rich dividends. Many handicapped people are ignored or shunned by society. A Christian taking the time to be a friend makes a definite impression. Friendship needs to be offered, not in sympathy for their condition but as a human contact of one person who genuinely cares about another. Friendship can be built in many different ways, but the key element is time. Time to talk, time to share feelings, and time to get acquainted are all important in building a friendship.

Another area, and probably the most important, is the need for love. Every person needs to love and to be loved. Our emotional lives are incomplete without love. Handicapped singles share this need. They intensely need love—Christian love—love which asks nothing in return. I find that when I reach out to love a person with a physical limitation, the returns are great. Jesus said in John 13:34-35, "A new commandment I give to you, that you love one another, even as I have loved you, that you also love one another. By this all men will know that you are My disciples, if you have love for one another." If you genuinely ask God to give you love for people, He will. This is His will, this is His commandment, and He can help us have a genuine Christian love for people.

There are many approaches to building this kind of relationship with a handicapped single. The first step is always to get acquainted. This takes time, it takes going out of your way, and it takes effort. When you meet a person who has a physical disability, as casually as possible, take the time to talk with him. Acknowledge his presence and ask how he is doing. Use any point of common interest that might come to your mind to start a conversation: the activity he is doing, the place where you met, the friends he's with, or the job he's doing. Find something positive with which to start a conversation. As quickly as appropriate, move from that point to his feelings about where he works or lives.

Ask questions that will allow him to share about his life. Sometimes it's appropriate to ask, or make a comment, "I notice that you seem to do very well with your situation." Allow him to answer and compliment him on the things that he is able to do. Don't be melodramatic. "How do you feel about life?" "How do you handle the frustration that must come as you live your daily life?"

In getting acquainted, let such persons tell you about their feelings. If they're open, let them share some life history. They might say, "I was injured in an accident" or "I was born like this" or "I was crippled by a disease." They want people to know how they came to be in this condition, and self-disclosure gets a burden off their chest.

Another way to get acquainted is to help them with some practical need. A handicapped person faces hundreds of barriers and hurdles each day that a normal person accomplishes with no effort at all. A simple opening of a door for a person in a wheelchair can be very frustrating. Getting in and out of a car can be an Olympic event. Writing a letter with cerebral palsy or some other debilitating disease can be exasperating and difficult. Offer your help wisely. Don't throw yourself at a handicapped person, but merely offer to assist in a quiet way without making a scene. If he refuses, just say, "You do that very well. If I can ever help, I'd be happy to." We can help with physical things such as transportation or with tasks such as reading or picking up a book or magazine for a person who is limited in travel. Sometimes taking the person to the store, a movie, or the doctor can be a small investment of time that yields great benefits in deepening the relationship and getting acquainted.

Investing casual time is of strategic importance in getting to know handicapped singles at a deeper human level. Casual activities such as going to a movie together, spending part of an afternoon or evening talking, or watching TV can help them relax and realize you genuinely care about them. Casual time provides an opportunity for a spiritual discussion.

Another way to make contact with singles is to join volunteer organizations which help them with the needs we've already mentioned. Many communities have a special assistance group which gives transportation, housework, and physical aid to people with disabilities. You might want to join one of those organizations. In many ways, we can simply look around and begin to see these people all around us in our universities, at work, and in our daily traffic pattern of life. Take the time to stop and say hello. You may be surprised at the response that you get.

In actually sharing the gospel there may be one major barrier. There may be a question in the back of the mind which must be dealt with. "Is my present situation because God willed it to be this way?" In other words, did God give me polio? Did God cause me to have this accident? In many people's minds, God is the cause of tragedy, or God is the cause of everything that happens. They conclude, "If I got sick or was injured, it's God's fault." We must spend time discussing the goodness of God, God's will, and God's plan for their lives. They may never be able to come to genuine trust in a God if they think He is cruel, heinous, and unforgiving. Take the time to discuss their beliefs with them. Talk about their situation. Help them to come to the realization that God does not cause everything that happens in the world.

An examination of Scripture can be very helpful. Romans 8:28 says, "And we know that God causes all things to work together for good to those who love God, to those who are called according to His purpose." Notice that it does not say that God causes all things. It does not say that everything that happens in our lives is God's will. It does say that after a life is given to God, God is big enough and strong enough to work in that life and to cause

71

all the things that have happened to somehow work out for good. This concept can set many people free from a fear of God.

Remember that many people's image of God comes not from the word of God, but from society, the media, and their own conclusions about life. A good biblical foundation here will be worth its weight in gold. Use their experience as they share with you to be a bridge from their lives to an understanding of the gospel. Help them see that, although they've had difficulties, God has watched over their lives. They are alive and have been given the gift of life by God.

Help them to see their need. If they are not Christians, they need to see they have sinned and are separated from God. Clearly explain the gospel—that Jesus is the Son of God, that He came to die for our sins, that He rose from the grave, and is the risen Lord—and help them understand that they must repent of sin as part of turning to belief in Christ. Invite them to respond by accepting Christ.

I find it helpful to offer assistance in a prayer of salvation. Many people are afraid to pray. They are afraid that they'll say the wrong thing or that you will think they are ignorant or immature. To solve these problems, I offer to lead them in a prayer of salvation and repentance. Do this phrase by phrase so that they can follow you. It's best to go through the prayer completely in a discussion format before you actually lead them in the prayer. A good way to do this is to say, "I know a prayer that expresses the things we've talked about. If you would like, you could pray this prayer after me. It goes like this. . . ."

Explain the prayer and ask if they would like to pray that prayer. If the answer is yes, then lead them phrase by phrase, allowing them to repeat after you. Stress that it's the sincerity of the heart that God observes, not the way they say the prayer. After they have prayed, seeking repentance and faith of salvation, assure them that God has heard their prayer and that they have begun the first step of a new life of obedience to Christ. I encourage you to include the handicapped single adults in your ministry. They need Christ, want Christ, and will be effective resources in sharing Christ with other handicapped singles, as well as with others they meet.

Part III
Locations of Single Adults

13

Condominiums and Apartments

KEN MORRIS, JR.

The apartment/condominium is a housing concept custom-made for a single life-style. Privacy and freedom are available for a minimum investment of maintenance, time, and money. Within these clustered units reside a constantly changing pool of potential relationships. Also, singles often find an atmosphere which affirms their singleness and does not question their marital status.

The vast majority of singles in our nation now live in apartments, condominiums, or some form of multiunit housing. Until we learn how to penetrate these hives of assorted humanity, we will not effectively reach the expanding single population of our society. Failure to develop strategies and means to minister to those living in apartments and condominiums is to write off future generations growing up in an increasingly urbanized world.

A People-Focused Mind-set

Jesus trained disciples. He challenged them to reshape their thinking, their values, and their direction in life. He did not develop programs as much as He sought to put Himself and the changed lives of His disciples in contact with others. As we seek ways to evangelize singles, there must be a people-focused mind-set which puts emphasis on reaching out through singles whose lives have been changed by Jesus Christ. This people-focused mind-set takes form in a program or strategy which places people, equipped to minister, in touch with others. It does not recruit people who crank out a program and expect it to work for them. Rather, the programs and activities become "bridges" connecting the Christian single with the non-Christian single.

A people-focused ministry is biblically based and the most effective approach to ministry among singles. The relational needs of most singles are a dominant factor in their decision making. Activities will not keep them around if there are no persons attending whom they perceive as potential friends. Thus, any ministry to singles in apartments or condominiums should begin with a team or core group who are spiritually and socially healthy: a group who will take initiative with others, seek to build genuine relationships, and maintain a firm conviction that Jesus reaches people through "His people."

A Ministry Cycle[1]

The following outline is best viewed as a cycle rather than a formula with a beginning and an end. It describes a process that should be repeated over and over again as you invest yourself in God's creative work among singles.

Preparation

Communicating vision. From the very start, challenge your church or group with a vision for reaching out to singles in apartments and condominiums. Help them to visualize how they can be a part of God's solution to the existing needs.

Gathering the facts. Research the apartments and condominiums in your community. Ask questions such as: What kind and how many apartments/condos are there? Are there singles in them? If so, what kind of singles and how many? How many of my current members, particularly singles, already live in these units?

Compile a list of needs you see among the singles in your area, especially among those living in the complexes you've researched. Also, gather information on various resources available to you such as personnel (and the time they can commit to the ministry), finances, space, and existing community services.

Establishing open lines of communication with management.[2]
Be ready and willing to invest time regularly communicating

and listening to feedback. This is important for establishing credibility and providing a context where you can work out misunderstandings or problems instead of being asked to leave.

Converting research into goals.[3] Don't do this alone! Gather your team or core group and together review the information you have compiled. Work toward group ownership of goals.

Determine the type(s) of singles you will serve and which complexes they can be found in. Take into consideration where some of your singles already live and who is willing to be a part of this outreach. (Having someone involved who also lives in the complex is a great advantage.) At least one should be in terms of a "bridging" activity or program. Make sure all goals are measurable!

Implementation

Continuously develop and train the core group. These people are key to the effectiveness of the ministry. They are the ones being placed alongside those without Christ. Apart from their spiritual vitality, the various programs and activities will resemble those of any other organization. The group must be stimulated to continue growing in their personal walk with God and discipleship.

The goals chosen must be regularly reviewed together and prayed for. If necessary, specialized training should be given for achieving specific goals. Accountability and affirmation should be a part of the group's dynamics. Be sure to include some "fun times" to keep the group from becoming too tense.

Carry out "bridging" activities. "Bridging" means the gospel is shared between persons brought together through some activity. An evangelistic emphasis is not dependent on the activity, but in the actions of those involved (whether they are seeking to share the gospel). For example, my involvement in organizing a community-wide wallyball league (not "church sponsored") has proven to be a much more effective "evangelistic" effort than a weekly Bible study we have.

"Bridging" means becoming an opportunist. "Conduct yourselves with wisdom toward outsiders, making the most of the opportunity" (Col. 4:5). We don't always need to create our own programs. Often there are already activities and organizations in the community or complex which appeal to those we are seeking to reach. If appropriate, get involved and let them provide a natural context for meeting people.

Being an opportunist also means taking advantage of "small" encounters: riding on the elevator, taking the trash out at the same time a neighbor does, meeting in the parking lot, etc. All of these "small" encounters can be opportunities to make a comment which can sow a seed for future discussion.

"Bridging" means serving the specific needs of others. We are called to serve and express genuine concern in the name of Jesus. How we do this is limited only by the number of human needs and our own sensitivity to them: through a kind note, helping someone move, inviting someone over for dinner, listening to the pains of a broken heart, or sponsoring a series of brunch/seminars covering basic life issues. Serving is the gospel in action!

"Bridging" means being a friend. Most people (especially singles) are always looking for a friend, but very few are willing to be one. This is a critical aspect of bridging. It almost always demands that the Christian be the initiator. The character of God's love is aggressive. He loved first, and now we are to love as He does. Take initiative with the singles you meet!

"Bridging" means special events. These events can create a sense of community, bring people together, and give them a common shared experience. Special events can range from a Fourth of July picnic, a Christmas tree-trimming party, a sports activity, a special worship service, or any activity which draws a large segment of the singles you are targeting. Make sure you include some singles who live in the targeted complex in the planning, even if they are not yet Christians.

"Bridging" means visibility in the community. Be willing to get involved in community concerns. Also, consider using posters, fliers, direct mailing, a monthly newsletter (either church sponsored and/or one that gives community news), or newspaper ads and articles. A logo on all your publicity can help your church or singles group become more easily recognized.

"Bridging" means a long-term commitment. Reaching those in an apartment or condominium complex cannot be done over a period of weeks or even months. There must be a sense of calling and commitment to this type of ministry from which endurance can be drawn. Relationships need time to grow, and we must be willing to give them our time.

Evaluation

Inside, looking out. Regularly evaluate goals and activities with those in your core group. However, evaluation is useful only when it results in taking definite steps of action. At least three possible actions you should consider are: to alter, to discontinue, or to intensify.[4]

Outside, looking in. Listen to those you are seeking to reach. How do they perceive what you are doing? Choose three or four non-Christian singles with whom you are well acquainted and ask if they would serve on a community relations-type committee. Keep them informed. Meet with them regularly (perhaps every three months?) to discuss what they observe about the church's ministry.

What Now?

The situation cannot be ignored! Singles are packed into apartments and condominiums in nearly every town and city across our nation. It is time we boldly go forward with a faith that takes risks for the sake of God's kingdom!

---

1. *Reaching Multifamily-Housing Residents: A Process Plan* (Atlanta: Home Mission Board, 1982).

2. *Ministry to Multifamily Housing Residents Manual* (Atlanta: Home Mission Board, 1982), pp. 13-18.

3. Edward R. Dayton and Ted W. Engstrom, *Strategy for Leadership* (Old Tappan, N.J.: Fleming H. Revell Co., 1979), pp. 51-68.

4. *Reaching Multifamily-Housing Residents: A Process Plan*, p. 5.

14

Military Bases

MILTON O. TYLER

There is no greater untapped resource of singles than on the nearest United States military installation. Yet many churches fail to realize the tremendous potential for evangelism that can be found on a typical military base. Not only is this where converts can be found, but it is also a source for finding Christian single adults who can be very effective volunteer workers.

Many of the singles in the armed services were at one time very involved in youth programs in local churches. Most of these singles have unlimited potential with various talents, and they inwardly yearn to be used in the Lord's work. Since the majority of these singles are young, there is also a vast reservoir of energy and creativity available to local congregations who can find the formula for involving military singles in their local church. Although some were reared in churches back home, they have not been encouraged to be active in a local congregation since coming on active duty. So in the military there can be found, in the truest sense, single adults who are resource and recipients for revival.

All types of singles may be found in the military. However, the largest group is the young, never-married single.

In order for a church to reach a single adult who is in the military, it is vital that a congregation understand who this person is. What are his or her needs? What is this temporary citizen of our community like? Is he like the stereotype we have of the hard-driving, wild-living, military person? There are important questions that a congregation must answer if they would have an effective ministry of love to the military. It seems to me that a church will never be able to successfully reach military singles unless the stereotype is replaced by viewing these young people as the boy or girl next door. The fact is, that's who they are. It is only as a church sincerely opens wide its doors of love to young soldiers, airmen, and sailors that there can be a Spirit-led church evangelistic outreach to the military. If we would seek to reach for Christ the young single in the armed forces, what do we need to understand about him/her?

The military single is usually serving on a base far away from his/her home. What an opportunity this provides the church to reflect how God cares for those who are lonely! Similar to a college student away from home, the military single often lives in a cramped room in a barracks located in a strange city far from parents, loved ones, and hometown friends. This is especially difficult on Christmas, Easter, Thanksgiving, and other family-centered holidays. Loneliness is certainly one of the situations that a local church should consider in their attempt to minister to military singles.

The church must further understand that this young prospect often is just out of high school or college. The reasons for enlisting in the service vary. Some enter the military because they are unsuccessful in finding a job that they feel has a future. Others choose the military because of the opportunity to learn a particular trade or to earn enough money to go to college. Still others choose the service because their goal is to be a military noncommissioned commissioned officer. These are singles who plan to spend a minimum of twenty years in the military service or until retirement.

For most of these young singles, this is their first time to truly be in charge of their own destiny. Some left home because of bad relationships with their parents, while others experience periods of mild depression because they miss their families so much. On Sunday morning there is now no one to tell them to get up and get ready for church. This new freedom is a great time of growth which can either be a curse or a blessing. What a wonderful time this can be for the church to make available its ministry.

Perhaps the strongest need of the young military single is to meet other singles of the opposite gender. The church is a natural place for this to happen in a wholesome environment. Singles like to be with other singles and to meet others who share the same needs. Local churches often miss reaching young military people by not advertising their singles' activities on military posts.

The church can also meet a tremendous need of armed forces singles by making available the opportunity to be invited for dinner on holidays like Thanksgiving and Christmas. Some churches have found an "adopt an airman/soldier" program to be very effective. In this program, families are encouraged to sign up to have one or more singles in their home for a holiday dinner. At the same time, singles are encouraged to sign up if they wish to have dinner with a church family. The church outreach director then assigns singles on the list to specific families. The family is given information on how to contact the single on the base and the responsibility to issue an invitation. Often the family also agrees to furnish transportation. This can be an opportunity to involve families, who before did very little in the church, in an ongoing ministry with their adopted military single. It can evolve into a ministry of singles being invited to family events and church activities by their sponsoring family. This can certainly be a blessing to the young serviceman far away from home on Christmas and Thanksgiving.

There is no group of singles more mobile and transient than the military. Their need is to quickly get involved in local activities. Unlike his/her civilian counterpart, the military single will seldom be at any given station more than three years. This creates a problem in that if the young soldier is to get involved in a local church, he has only a limited time to do it. This is why some military people are hesitant to join a local church. The reasoning used is, "Why move my membership or join the church since I will be here only for a limited time?" Therefore, it is very beneficial for a church to try to reach military singles as soon as possible after they arrive on their new base.

What then can your church do to reach military singles? This obviously is a complex question. The answer depends on many factors. Let me suggest several approaches that your church may choose to utilize as you seek to reach single military personnel.

Perhaps the most important step to be taken is for your church staff, especially the pastor, to meet and get to know the chaplains on the military base. This is vital if your church military ministry is to be successful. Many pastors fail to understand that the chaplain is a home missionary from his/her denomination. The base chapel is set up not as a rival church (there is no membership in the chapel), but as a mission preaching station and for the purpose of supporting the local church. The installation staff chaplain will be happy to inform you of the opportunities for your church at his base. Many chaplains will even make available literature from your church to personnel on base. But most of all, let the chaplains know of your concern for singles. Often singles will ask the chaplain where good single church programs are located. The chaplain will, in most cases, give your church's publicity and name if you have kept in touch with the base chapel.

Another important factor is the groups already ministering there on the base. On many bases, one can find a number of parachurch groups who are conducting Bible studies, discipleship courses, and other Christian ministries. Many of these groups also encourage their participants to attend a local church. These groups, such as the Officers' Christian Fellowship and the Navigators, have very effective Bible study ministries and encourage their members to join and be active in Bible-believing churches. A local church could easily inform these groups of their ministry to singles, and perhaps find a new resource in reaching military personnel.

Publicity is another very vital tool that can be used in reaching military singles. Not only should the publicity specifically invite military singles, but it must also clearly state what benefit this would give a single who attends. It also must be in a place where the young soldier will see it. Posters can be printed in the base paper or in locations off base where the military single visits. Publicity needs to be eye-catching and attractive.

Special events for singles is another way to reach military prospects. This can be in the form of concerts, seminars, or weekend retreats. Other events might be dinners with special speakers (such as Fellowship of Christian Athletes) or seasonal activities, such as Christmas caroling, Easter sunrise service, or mission outings. Many military singles will be most likely to respond first to a special event. Then if they feel the church really cares for singles, they will come back to the worship service and Sunday School class.

One important suggestion I would make to a church is to offer transportation for singles to church activities. Many young military singles do not have automobiles. Often they will go to any activity which takes them away from the dorm and does not cost a lot of money.

What about the church that is not near a military installation? Is it possible for this church to minister to military singles? The answer is absolutely yes. Check the nonresident rolls and find out where the young men and women are now stationed who once were active in the church membership. A survey of the membership can also discover others who are away in the military. Many of these nonresident singles would be happy to hear from their home church. How welcome a cassette tape of a worship service or of the old Sunday School class would be to a single stationed on some remote radar site in Alaska or on a ship in the Indian Ocean. Consistent contact with these military singles could be meaningful.

Military singles desperately need the church. These are young people with many needs, yet they have much to offer. There is one major difference between the military single and the civilian single. Because of the nature of the military singles' job when they are reached for Christ, they become worldwide missionaries. Their next assignment could be Europe, Japan, the Philippine Islands, or some other foreign mission field. If motivated and discipled properly by the local church, these singles can assist and help our foreign missionaries by becoming foreign missionaries themselves. Truly, the local church needs to catch a vision of the military single as both a resource and a recipient for revival.

15

Nursing Homes

HORACE L. KERR

A nursing home may seem to be a very unlikely place to witness. The stereotypical resident, sick and senile, would seem an unlikely prospect for evangelistic effort.

On the other hand, a nursing home might seem to be a good place to witness if you subscribe to the "foxhole" theory of one quickly turning to God under adverse circumstances. Surely the person facing an imminent end to this life would eagerly accept an invitation to a better life in the hereafter!

Both of these suppositions are based on false assumptions with regard to nursing home residents. To be an effective witness to persons in nursing homes, one needs to be more aware of the realities of these institutions and some of the characteristics of those who live there.

Most nursing home residents are older persons. The singles to whom you might witness there will most likely be older persons—senior adults. So you need not only an understanding of the institutionalized single person but also of older persons and the effects (or lack of effects) of the aging process. Obviously everything you need to know about these target persons cannot be written in one brief chapter. However, we can deal with some basic understandings which will be helpful.

First, you should recognize that a variety of persons live in nursing homes. There may even be some younger singles there, convalescing from an illness or with some chronic conditions which may keep them there. Single adults with no family to assist them may be more likely candidates for institutional care. Expect to find many levels of physical ability or disability. Not all residents are bed patients.

Do not expect all residents to be senile—not even all of the older persons. Studies reveal that only 2 to 3 percent of all institutionalized older persons are clinically senile. Many do exhibit senile behavior which is enhanced by patronizing or dictatorial personnel.

Persons in nursing homes are not outcasts. Granted that some should not be there, the majority are there because of their need for that level of medical care. Recognize them as persons with capabilities and sensitivities. They are persons, human beings, God's creation, in His image, and deserving of being treated with dignity.

The older persons are not there because they are old. They are there, hopefully, only because they have physical needs for which neither they nor their families can provide. It is a myth that the end result of the aging process is physical and mental infirmity. You have only to look about you to see that most older persons continue to live in uninstitutionalized settings.

This information should help you understand who is in the nursing home and why.

To relate to nursing home residents as effective witnesses, we need also to understand the quality of life in such an institution. Realize that it is the person's home. That is why we use the term "resident" rather than patient. Many factors determine the quality of life experienced by persons in a given home. They include physical arrangements, food, training and disposition of personnel, availability and type of activities, and opportunities to be outside the home. Another factor is the sociability and general attitude of the resident himself/herself. Many nursing homes would receive a low grade on provision for quality of life, even some which would receive high marks for quality of care. It is important to note that where these recipients of witnessing live impacts greatly their feeling about the quality of their lives. They need outside support to enhance the quality of their lives.

Turn now from general understandings of nursing home residents to look at some potential barriers to your witnessing effort. Some, having come to the state of being institutionalized, feeling shut out from the world and having their lives come to a negative end, will look on your offer of eternal, quality life as pie-in-the-sky or another scheme for which they will not fall. Similarly, others will be so affected by their physical condition that they will not be concerned about the spiritual. Both of these groups will raise the question of why God allows such an ending or suffering if He does indeed exist. Some will feel God is punishing them and that He will not accept them. There will be a few whose mental condition will make it almost impossible for you to know if they are receiving the message you seek to give them.

Environmental barriers may need to be overcome. There is little possibility for privacy in many homes unless the resident has a private room.

With this background of information, consider some approaches to witnessing to single adults in nursing homes. It is very evident that a cultivative approach must be used here even more than with persons in more normal living arrangements. As has been indicated, the trust level of many residents is quite low. Trust in you as a sincere, well-meaning person will come as you cultivate that person's friendship. Trust in what you say and willingness to hear God's Word as you read and quote it comes after the person trusts you.

Dependability is a characteristic for which the resident will look as you seek to cultivate his/her friendship. Being there, calling, writing when you say you will and doing what you say you will do is very important to that person's ability to trust you.

The good Samaritan approach is also important here. Although the biblical account of the story doesn't include witnessing to the man in need, the approach of first meeting basic needs before confronting with higher needs is a valid one. You will not be involved in meeting the resident's physical needs except as an encourager, but there are many things you can do for him/her. They include running errands, writing letters, reading, taking her/him on an excursion out of the nursing home (if permissible), and many other neighborly acts.

To become a witnessing friend, build anticipation into your relationship. Give your new friend something to look forward to.

Through these approaches, you help the resident focus on quality of life more than on length of life.

Your approach in sharing the gospel, the good news of salvation, to the nursing home resident should be a natural part of this building of relationships. Scripture passages used should be the positive promises of God rather than being heavy on the negative, although it is a fact that "the wages of sin is death" (Rom. 6:23). These persons are, for the most part, living in the negative, especially if they are without Christ. They need the hope and assurance that comes with being rightly related to God. They will more nearly come to that relationship in a salvation experience if you hold out that hope and assurance through the promises found in the Scriptures. As they trust you, they will hear God's Word from you, and the Holy Spirit will work in their hearts.

Be careful in your prayer with your new friend not to raise expectations which, unrealized, would be a barrier to his/her acceptance of the truths of God which you share.

Lead the single adult in the nursing home to commitment to Christ as you would a person in any other environment. However, there is a word of caution. If you have built a helpful relationship, the resident may so wish to please you that she/he will give verbal assent to your appeal without having had a real experience. Be careful in your leading to see signs of understanding of what you are suggesting and what God is requiring.

Follow-up is extremely important in witnessing to an institutionalized person. Assurance and growth come with continuing contacts. Consider building a support group of Christians in the nursing home. This is especially needed by the single adult who may not have the natural support of a family.

It should be obvious in the approaches suggested here that single adults will be the most effective witnesses to single adult residents of nursing homes. Christian singles in nursing homes have an even greater opportunity in witnessing to their peers.

A nursing home really is a good place to witness for Christ. Wholeness of life is hardly dreamed of by many residents. We know that it is possible through Christ even for those who may be physically impaired.

16

University Campuses

JOYCE ASHCRAFT

"Lift up your eyes, and look on the fields, that they are white for harvest" (John 4:35).

Every year thousands of students enroll in the nation's colleges and universities. These institutions are the training centers for young adults as they pursue a course of study that will prepare them for their life's work. This is the place where life goals, values, and dreams are explored by students. Included in this exploration is the question of God and how He will impact their lives.

Possibly the location that is "ripest for harvest" among single adults is the campus. Nowhere else are singles gathered in such large numbers for the purpose of shaping and changing their lives. They come to the classroom with the intent of building a new, independent life for themselves. For many of these young adults, it may be the last time their hearts and minds will be open enough to hear the gospel. The need is an urgent one.

However, the traditional stereotypes of students must be changed. No longer is the college dorm student in the majority. New trends in higher education are leading us away from a resident college and into a new pattern of university and college life. More and more students are attending community colleges and remaining at home or moving into apartments near the campus. They are caught in the whirlwind rush of our American life-style and live many hours of their lives in a car or on public transportation, caught up in the impersonal mobile society found there. Though the commuter colleges offer more students a quality academic education, they do not offer the social interaction that can be found at resident institutions. Thus, the idea of life-style evangelism becomes much harder to communicate but imperative if the idea of who Jesus is is going to penetrate the heart of these students. Many do not get close to even one new friend in the course of their college career.

One of the common errors in ministering to college singles is the idea that since they can be found in such large numbers in one geographic location, mass evangelism techniques can be used effectively. This could not be further from the truth. These students need a personal touch. They need someone who cares about them as individuals to reach out to them and tell them how Jesus Christ can change their life—not just while they are in college but for their lifetime.

College students are emotionally up. They are climbing the ladder. For most, the idea that they are single adults is a foreign concept. Perhaps a more correct term would be "not yet married." For many, the idea of singleness has a negative connotation. They believe that being referred to as single means they have chosen a single life-style for the rest of their lives. This is not true for students. The vast majority of students are aiming toward marriage and family roles for their future and may spend a large portion of their time while in college pursuing the fulfillment of this goal.

Another complicating factor in evangelism on the college campus is economics. More and more students are having to work at least part of the day to be able to afford their education. So, instead of the full-time college student of twenty years ago, there are students whose lives are fragmented by academic study, work, family ties, etc. This means they are distracted from some of the life-forming processes that are usually accomplished in college. However, it is still time for the decisions and direction to be made and set. Thus, it is at this point of need that we must communicate if we are to experience revival of the college and university campuses of our nation.

There are four major areas of need for the non-Christian student. These are areas which must be dealt with if we are to experience revival on the campus. Though these areas are separate, they build on each other. All four needs must be met for students to come to know Christ. Let us take a look at each of these four needs: relationship, message, opportunity for decision, and follow-up.

Relationship

In spite of the busyness of the student, relationship is often their major need. Many times they feel isolated in the crowd. They are longing to meet others and know that the things they are experiencing and feeling are OK. They need the opportunity to dialogue with each other about those major decisions they are facing. Students need to know that someone cares enough about them to invest time in them.

For many students, the idea that someone outside their family would care deeply about them is a new concept. Even though they have experienced close peer relationships in their high school years, most have not thought extensively about these relationships. The newness of college life will accentuate both the need and the desire for close relationships.

Revival will not come to the campuses unless this need is met. A relationship with Jesus Christ becomes even more believable and appealing when shared from someone who cares as opposed to someone who is merely sharing facts. The relationship between the Christian and non-Christian is a very important element in sharing the message of Jesus Christ.

The Message

Building relationships will not in and of itself bring revival to the campus. More and more of today's students have never really heard the message of good news. Though they may have grown up around the corner from a church, they have never heard that Jesus Christ died for them, making possible a right relationship with God which can be personally experienced. The concept of God is not a foreign concept. However, the idea of a personal relationship with God is a new concept for most non-Christian students. Thus, if there is to be revival on campus, relationships must be built and the message must be clear.

The Opportunity to Decide

The message must bring with it an opportunity to decide. Simply hearing the message is not enough. Students need to be personally confronted with the opportunity to accept or reject the gospel message. Unless they are brought to the point of personal decision, they will not personalize the message. This very fact makes personal relationships even more important. Most students who are pressed to the point of decision by someone who has not taken time to get to know them will read this as aggression. Many times they will never "hear" the message because they are so busy rejecting that aggressiveness. It seems that the relationship with the one sharing is very important to hearing and deciding on the message.

Follow-Up

Follow-up, too, is important if we are to experience revival on the campus. Whether the student accepts or rejects the gospel, follow-up must occur. If he rejects the gospel, he must not be given the opportunity to affirm his beliefs about "Christians" and "the church." Whether or not he receives Christ, he deserves the opportunity to experience the love of God. His only avenue for experiencing this love will be through relationship with others.

If he accepts Christ, the student needs opportunity to grow. He needs to know that the point of decision has begun a long journey that will last the rest of his life. He needs help in getting started on the journey. Again, this must be done in relationship—either one-on-one or in small groups. This needs to include training in basic Christian disciplines as well as an opportunity to dialogue about his daily Christian life and what he is learning day by day.

Resources for Revival

The major resource for revival on the campus is on the campus itself. Students understand each other better than anyone else can. Thus, revival on a campus is going to come through students. The implications of this statement are great. If we are to experience revival on the college campus, we must mobilize the task force which we have at our fingertips. Christian college students must be trained in evangelism. They must know how to present the message of Christ to their peers. Thus, evangelism training sessions are a must.

Christian students must catch the vision. They need to realize that if an impact is made on their campus, it will not come from the work of paid evangelists alone but through their zeal and commitment to the task.

Finally, Christian students need to take the risk. They need to actively seek to be involved in the lives of their peers. And, one by one, our campuses will be won to Christ. Students must learn to say with Paul, "I have become all things to all men, that I may by all means save some" (1 Cor. 9:22).

17

Ethnic Neighborhoods

HERMAN RIOS

There are 232,000,000 people in the United States. It is estimated that 132,000,000 are ethnics—people from all over the world coming to the United States. They come for education, employment, a better way of life. Among these ethnics are many singles. They are here to stay, and more will be coming each year.

Some of the more interesting statistics among ethnics in America are as follows:[1]

- Eighty-two percent of the immigrants in 1980 came from Latin American and Asia.
- Chicago is the second largest Polish city in the world, second only to Warsaw.
- Los Angeles has a Hispanic population larger than any country in Central America.
- Los Angeles is the Vietnamese capital of America. It is the second largest Korean city in the world, the second largest Hispanic city in the western hemisphere, and the second largest Salvadorian city in the world.
- Miami is the second largest Cuban city in the world, second only to Havana.
- New York is the second largest Puerto Rican city, second to San Juan.
- Daily newspapers are printed in more than forty-five different languages in America.
- There are some 11.1 million people in the United States who speak a language other than English at home.
- Between 1980 and 1983, over 525,000 refugees entered the United States.
- The state of Michigan has the largest Arab population in the country with 250,000 people of Arabian ancestry in Detroit alone.

Obviously, a significant percentage of each of these figures would be single adults. The conclusion is that we cannot attempt to reach single adults in America and ignore those singles of ethnic ancestry.

The future political leaders of Third World countries are now in America preparing for the role they will play, and many of them are single. Ethnic singles basically have the same needs as American singles. They face many of the same problems and pressures.

We in America have a great opportunity to become "love in action" to ethnic singles.

We *must recognize* that ethnic singles are here. Ethnic singles are found in any community where there are colleges and universities or factories and even in rural areas.

We cannot afford to take anything for granted when ministering to ethnic singles. Even though they have many of the same needs as American singles, there are differences.

We *must realize* that ethnics are people for whom Jesus died. They are people, not second-class citizens. We must approach them as we would approach someone in our own family.

The ethnic people consist of more than 200 ethnic groups and 495 American Indian tribes in the United States. Including the undocumented, there are approximately 23 million Hispanics, making the United States the fifth largest Spanish-speaking country in the world; 3.5 million Asian and Pacific Islanders; 1.4 million American Indians; almost one million Chinese; over 700,000 Filipinos; over 700,000 Japanese; over 350,000 Koreans; and 7.5 million internationals in the United States.[2] Many of these are single.

We as Christians *must see the reality* of winning ethnic singles to Jesus Christ. Ethnic singles can be found anywhere—some ethnics can be identified by physical features, while others cannot. As you go, be aware of ethnic people.

As you continue to look at the total community to identify ethnic singles, be aware of ethnic restaurants, ethnic gift shops, ethnic churches, ethnic clubs and organizations, theaters that show foreign language movies, and ethnic barrios or colonies.

A survey of these areas and ethnic communities will help identify ethnic singles. The findings will determine the type of witnessing approach to follow.

We as Christians *must be aware of the role* of ethnic. We must strive for a more accurate view of ethnic singles. As we look at ethnic singles, we will realize that in the United States in every group we will find more than one generation here. At least be aware of the major subgroups.

There are those who are "effectively assimilated" in the language, life-styles, and social economic level of the community where they live. There are ethnic singles who are "partially assimiliated" and others who are "effectively segregated."

Ethnic singles who are "effectively assimilated" have effectively assimilated into life-styles where they live in the United States. They may or may not have been born in the United States. They speak English well and in some cases, it may be the only language spoken. They will be greatly influenced by the community where they live. They do not wish or like to be segregated. They already attend schools, businesses, recreation centers, theaters as anyone else in town. This individual can be effectively reached for the Lord Jesus Christ.

The "partially assimilated" ethnic single is able to function in more than one life-style and in more than one language. A bilingual approach should be considered in reaching partially assimilated ethnic singles. Some singles in this group will move toward "effectively assimilated," while others will never move from "partially assimilated."

The "effectively segregated" ethnic single is segregated by language, culture, and social economics. Some are in this category by choice and others by necessity. These singles are difficult to reach from an English-speaking congregation. Over three million people in the United States do not speak English well; another 1.2 million do not speak English at all.[3] A congregation of their mother language and culture is usually most effective in reaching the "effectively segregated" ethnic singles.

Some "effectively segregated" ethnic singles might assimilate to "partially" or "effectively," depending on age, education, skills and length of time in the United States.

In evangelizing singles in ethnic neighborhoods, keep some basic suggestions in mind.[4]

- Pray for the leadership of the Holy Spirit.
- Accept ethnics as equals; do not look down on them.
- Become a friend.
- Relax and be yourself.
- Identity is important; let ethnic singles know what you represent.
- Give some orientation to ethnics. Do not take anything for granted. Many ethnics may not be familiar with the way you worship.
- Speak slowly; do not speak low; give sufficient time to be understood.
- Do not be afraid to share the gospel.
- There is no room for argument and disrespect.
- You may need to take someone with you who is bilingual to help you share effectively.

As the ethnic population increases, our responsibility increases. "According to *The Global Report to the President,* there is a possibility that more than 30 percent of those born in third-world countries will migrate to the U.S. The Central-American crisis is already impacting the nation. The Hong Kong Treaty of 1997 will bring thousands to our shores."[5] As we reach out to single adults and as we equip singles to evangelize others, we must "not neglect to show hospitality to strangers [sojourners]" (Heb. 13:-2).

---

1. *The Mandate,* vol. 1, no. 1 (September, 1984), Arcadia, California. (*The Mandate* is a publication of Houston '85, The National Convocation on Evangelizing Ethnic America.)
2. Ibid.
3. Ibid.
4. These suggestions are taken from *Guide for Establishing Ethnic Congregations,* Language Missions Department, Home Mission Board, SBC, Atlanta, Georgia.
5. *Communique,* vol. 1, no. 2 (November, 1984), Atlanta, Georgia. (*Communique* is a publication of the Language Missions Division of the Home Mission Board, SBC.)

18

Affluent Neighborhoods

BARBARA MCNEIR

Churches in affluent neighborhoods have the same challenge before them as their sister churches in the suburb or in the inner city. The challenge is found in Christ's parting words to His disciples. The church is to reach out to everyone, everywhere, no matter whether their name is listed in Dun and Bradstreet or on an overdrawn checking account. However, affluence can sometimes compound the problem the church may have in reaching the wealthy single adult.

One of the problems is the number of options that are available to the affluent single for the use of investment of his money, possessions, or influence. Some of these options are attractive because they cost a great deal and are an immediate means of identification with wealth. Some of the options are attractive because of the prestige of being seen with the right people in the right place at the right time. Some churches have the distinction of being that kind of place. Those churches have the responsibility of privilege to avoid any "negative press" for Christianity.

There is nothing inherently wrong with having money. But the Bible is clear on the perils of loving money more than God. The first danger is the short-term high that affluence can give. There is the tendency to forget about God and the fact that the power to get wealth is a gift from Him.

A second danger is the growth of the natural sin to desire more and more, either through accumulation or hoarding—no matter if land or shoes or marbles. This naturally leads to an attitude of constant care and anxiety about wealth, which then results in meaninglessness of life. The pressure to perform while minimizing the reality of the burden of wealth can create real tension in one's life.

The most powerful temptation for the affluent single adult is to be lured away from a faith in God and away from a realization of the need for a personal relationship with God through Jesus Christ.

In order for the church to reach the affluent single adult, the church must offer something that is attractive and interesting enough to make it worthwhile to give up some other options that are available and adopt a new priority. The church has the challenge of leading the affluent single to see his or her need for the Father first, and then the family. Most people have the attitude of "What's in it for me?" And the best person to answer that for the affluent single is another affluent single. They are able to communicate verbally and nonverbally.

One suggestion for involving the affluent single as both resource and recipient of revival is to have the Christian singles of your church invite two or three non-Christian singles from within their circle of influence to a dinner party. This could be held at a well-known restaurant in a private dining or at the country club or the Junior League. The guests would be the financial responsibility of the Christian single and could be neighbors, business associates, leisuretime friends, fraternal brothers or sisters, community associates, etc. The additional costs for room rental, flowers, engraved invitations, gratuities, and honorarium are shared equally by the host and hostesses. The honorarium is for a great speaker, such as a public figure, an author, or a respected business person who is well known as a good speaker and who is a Christian.

After dinner, begin with some light entertainment, preferably provided by the singles themselves. If there is a soloist among the group, that person could share his or her testimony in song. At least two and no more than three (if a soloist is used) Christian singles could give their personal testimony (three to five minutes) about their relationship with God, putting the emphasis on how He has helped them reach/maintain their position of affluence. The singles need to be able to communicate the message that they recognize the burdens of wealth as well as the blessings. It is also important that the lives of these singles testify to their commitment of being Christlike in word, thought, and deed. Following the testimonies, the guest speaker shares for fifteen to twenty minutes how he or she depends on God in a personal, private, and public way. To close, the pastor or some other representative minister from the church gives a summary statement as to the plan and purpose of God to have a personal relationship with everyone. The pastor then asks permission to close with a prayer of praise and thanks to God for allowing this time of fellowship to let friends know that relationships are more important than things.

An alternative to this would be to have small dinners in homes or at the church just prior to the revival meeting, targeting specific groups: professionals, public figures, social elites. Then have a Christian representative of that group give a brief testimony before everyone goes to the revival together.

Many singles welcome the opportunity to show off their culinary skills. Invite a few friends over for a dine 'n dialogue evening on issues that are of interest/importance to single adults in today's society. "Pressure Points" is an evangelistic tool published by the Home Mission Board designed to create an atmosphere in which the Christian single can share his or her view of and value on a topic in a nonthreatening way. This could also be done over a Saturday morning cup of coffee, at the health club after a game of racquetball, or on the local jogging path.

The most effective way for a Christian single to witness to a non-Christian single is through his or her life-style. Relational witnessing is more likely to be received in a positive manner by the affluent than a direct approach on the basis of obvious need. The Christian single needs to get to know the non-Christian well enough to earn the right as well as the trust to talk about personal things at a deeper level without the fear of that person being one page or one book ahead of you. The affluent Christian needs to be able to pinpoint specific times in his or her life when God supplied a need that no amount of money could buy—a friend with whom to share a hurt or a joy who understands and/or shares the same value system, a youth minister who can communicate with a child on a level no parent can about real life issues, a group of people who like you for who you are rather than for what you own.

Only the affluent Christian single adult can explain to the affluent non-Christian single adult the concept of "profit and loss" in God's economy found in Matthew 16:26 or 19:21 or 19:29. (Don't forget Matthew was an expert on the tax laws!) The affluent single needs to recognize and accept God as the giver of all good gifts, including the ability to profit from wealth and to rejoice in its accumulation (Eccl. 5:19).

19

Low-Income Neighborhoods

TIMOTHY M. LARKIN

In looking to the task of evangelizing low-income singles, it will be important to understand the environment, stimulus, and identity of this group. Towards this purpose, we will limit our discussion to the single male or female between the ages of twenty to thirty-five who lives in inner urban centers on a fixed or survival income.

Jim is a single white male in his mid-twenties. He does not have a job, has been hospitalized many times for psychotic behavior, presently sleeps in the park along the Chicago lakefront, and eats at two free meal programs at the local Salvation Army and a local church. Jim has heard the gospel message many times and enjoys going to church. However, because of his inappropriate behavior and uncleanliness, Jim is seen as a problem within most institutions, including the church, rather than a welcomed individual. How does the church minister share the gospel, bringing about a spiritual awakening in the life of such a single?

Janet is a single parent with two children ages five and ten, from different broken relationships. She is on welfare and goes to class for her high school diploma. Her mother and grandmother are on the welfare rolls. She feels overwhelmed and will come to the church in time of need. She sends her children regularly to the church. However, she doesn't feel worthy or ready to engage in a Christian walk even though she continues to hear the gospel.

These two individuals give us a glimpse of the complex world of the low-income single. We cannot stereotype all low-income singles as alcoholics or a specific race or look to simple answers for the complex questions of their lives. The purpose of this chapter is to bring an understanding of low-income singles so that the spiritual issues for this group can be observed. The spiritual issues lead to needs for strategies that reveal Christ as the answer to the singles' spiritual questions.

Knowing some characteristics of low-income singles will provide us handles to understand the spiritual questions this group is asking. The low-income single lacks in many areas what more affluent single programs are built around. He lacks quality education, finances, social and communication skills. With these deficiencies, the single continues in fear, mistrust, cynicism, and apathy; the spiritual quest for faith, hope, peace, and joy are not pursued. The low-income single sees life as a succession of events, not a process. Thus a natural selfishness evolves whereby the single gets all he or she can from the event. A survival mentality exists. The goal is to survive *this day,* and the future is forgotten. How do we share a gospel that calls one to a life of growth or process? Consistency in an event-oriented life is not necessary, and behavior problems such as uncontrolled anger or additions are not processed or worked through because all that matters is the present. How do we present a God who loves us and wants us to grow and thus be fulfilled through a spiritual process culminating in a spiritual place called heaven?

Low-income singles seem to view the church as a place to "get" and to be used. The history of dependency for many singles creates a bitterness towards the church, and a struggle of "you owe me" and I owe you nothing begins. Satan desires to use their fear, bitterness, apathy, event crisis, and survival orientation so that they won't look at important eternal issues and present growth issues of well-being.

Let us now look at how the church and the Spirit-led individual can reach out to the low-income single. The church and the individual that seeks to evangelize the low-income single will need to expect to feel taken advantage of; in many cases one actually is taken advantage of. A call to this form of ministry is a call to emotional attacks, abusive language, and threats, as well as spiritual attacks.

The church can expect things to be missing and to feel violated. However, by weathering this storm, the church is investing in sharing the gospel message. The low-income single is used to being lost and not noticed, so the church will need to seek out the single. The interaction in filling a physical need such as food or clothing can be used to receive an address, and an opportunity to visit the single at home or on the street is created. Visitation, prayer, and setting up safe havens of service for the single are the keys to evangelizing this group. At the Uptown Baptist Church in Chicago, the clothing giveaway, the Monday hot meal program, and the Praise Night offering are places where the low-income single serves and is trusted with responsibility. We see Christ's example in these same areas in His interaction with the woman at the well, the seeking out of Zacchaeus, and the allowing of Mary Magdalene to wash His feet with expensive oil.

For a church to allow low-income singles to be a part of the life of the church takes a time commitment. The church begins "living" with the single so that the event-crisis life-style turns into a process of faith and hope through Christ. It has been my experience that it takes two years of discipleship and living with the single before a pattern of Spirit-led stability emerges.

Because the single is so used to crisis, it is sometimes his pattern to create crisis through mental breakdowns, chemical dependency binges, or fleeing the area. We understand that this is created from fear, and the opposite of fear is faith.

We can use the crisis as a chance to teach the single about faith and encourage steps of faith such as developing patience. The church now becomes a statement and example of hope. Hope is the one weapon that consistently defeats apathy. Since our hope is encompassed by our faith (Heb. 11:1), we have the wonderful gift of freedom and stability. Jeremiah 29:11 states that God has plans for us and that they are for our good. Then Jeremiah shares that the result of these plans is a future and a hope. So through the church's statement and example of hope, the single is brought to a position and freedom to choose. God loves us so much He allows us to say no.

The church must be willing to hear the single if he says no and allow the consequences to be felt by the single. Not that the church withholds love or coerces the single to act a certain way; however, actions such as those listed in Galatians 5:19-21 should not be allowed within the church. The church should be careful not to be enabling the survival system to flourish for the single. This will mean asking intoxicated individuals to choose between appropriate behavior or leaving a church service or activity. This may mean not bailing an individual out of jail. Discernment in such matters comes from the history of life together that the single has with the church or individual. Because of this history of relating to the church, the church understands patterns and accepts the single back as a demonstration of forgiveness when the single returns in quest of reconciliation.

An intervention for the church worker is the development of a primary relationship with the single. It has been noted how important the church is as part of the kinship system of the single.[1] Primary relationship building means one-on-one interaction. Males should minister to males and females should minister to female singles. This will help eliminate a sexual conquest agenda and provide a firm role model for the single as well as protect the ministering individual. Through this time of relating, the concerned Christian will see the needs that Satan is using to prevent the person from growing spiritually. This can be anything from obsessive thought to no place to stay. The ministering Christian can pray and try to meet these needs, then call the single to a higher understanding and point out the spiritual choices he or she is making. Another helpful intervention is to set up a structure of time, events, and choices so that the single begins exercising choice. The single has a tendency to say no to most things including God. This structure includes areas of daily living such as cleanliness and uncluttered apartments and what day the one-on-one Bible study will be held.

In conclusion, I want to emphasize the role the church and the ministering individual have in confirming the faith and encouraging the growth of the low-income single. This ranges from rebuking oppressive systems in the city to encouraging the low-income single not to live in apathy and fear. Just as we may not remember what we ate three days ago, we know that the food helped. The low-income single may not remember the spiritual truth you shared and structured for him to choose for his life three days ago; however, you can be assured it helped and you can experience the joy of sharing Jesus and His truths again.

---

1. Mansell Pattison, M.D.; Donald Detranciso, M.D.; Paul Wood, J.D.; Harold Frazier, M.D., and John Crowder, M.D. "A Psychosocial Kinship Model for Family Therapy," *American Journal of Psychiatry* 132:12, December 1975, pp. 1246-1251.

Part IV
Avenues to Single Adults For Revival

20
Church Weekday Ministry
MIKE CLAYTON

The telephone rings at the local church and the caller asks the following questions: "Do you have a single adult department? Will you tell me something about it? When do they meet? Who do they do? Where do they get together?" And these are the most common: "What are the single adults doing tonight?" or "What are the singles doing this weekend?" These are familiar questions put to churches today who are expressing a desire to reach, win, and minister to the needs of adult singles of any age.

These and other similar questions reflect an outward expression of one or more emotional, relational, social, psychological, or spiritual needs found among single adults. It doesn't matter whether they are widowed, divorced, or never married. There are some common factors that they all have, and the most important is that they need Jesus as their personal Savior and Lord of their life.

Most adults who are not married, for whatever reason, have a desire for activity. They want to be busy outside the confines of their four walls, so they seek entertainment, conversation, and fellowship with others. This need for acceptance and friends has made a multimillion dollar business out of attracting singles to physical fitness clubs, restaurants, bars, dating services, cruise trips, travel clubs, and a long list of various singles organizations.

The Sunday School is, of course, the chief organizational tool for reaching, teaching, winning, and developing single adults for Christ through the church. It should always be the hub of the ministry's wheel, with everything else as a spin-off from the Sunday School and everything else also pointing back to the Sunday School.

Weekday ministries are an extension of the outreach and need-meeting challenge of the Sunday School. It is through weekday ministries that churches can attempt to build opportunities of showing acceptance, providing entertainment, fellowship, friendship, and a sense of belonging all within the context of biblical principles.

It is important to note that weekday ministries, whatever they might be, should always have outreach and evangelism as primary purposes. Everything planned, prepared, and promoted should be used as an opportunity to reach out and include the outsider who is not part of the group or the church.

Ann Alexander Smith in her booklet *How to Start a Single Adult Ministry* gives a simple but very important formula for planning weekday ministries to reach and minister to adult singles. It is NEEDS + PEOPLE = PROGRAM. She also suggests that a sound single adult ministry takes into account the whole person.

Therefore, it is important to evaluate the needs, ages, reasons for singleness, and desires of the adult singles in your church before planning weekday ministry programs. But if these ministries are to be used as outreach and evangelism tools, then the same evaluation must be made of the singles within the city or the area surrounding the church. Often people are not reached because the program developed for ministry does not plan to reach the outsider.

The philosophy must be adopted that "everything we do involves outreach" if real evangelism and revival are to take place within the single adult program. Ministry activities throughout the week must be utilized as reaching agents and not only as filling the gap between Sundays for members.

So, as calendar planning is done, the insider and the outsider both must be considered. Both Christians and non-Christians are the target groups to whom weekday programs are to minister.

There needs to be a mixture of weekday activities within any given month or year. More importantly, there must be adequate balance in programming.

Spiritual growth, recreation, evangelism, missions, food, and entertainment are some basic categories that planned weekday ministries fall into. It is important to evaluate calendar scheduling to see that all areas are represented. There needs to be a healthy balance, always taking into consideration ministry to the member and outreach to the outsider. Variety is a key principle in planning.

Bible studies at the homes of members, apartment clubrooms, parks, or at the church facility are vital weekday programs. They should be topical studies that answer questions asked by single adults. The topics should be promoted in advance so they can attract members and guests alike. Food of some kind can also be served to aid in fellowship.

A one-night seminar or conference relating to a spiritual growth subject or an area of single adult need is also viable. These kinds of activities meet needs and answer questions.

Volleyball tournaments, roller skating nights, softball games, lake days, picnics, flag football games, horseback riding, and other forms of recreation help to provide Christian fellowship. These weekday activities are wonderful opportunities to build friendships and to expose friends, relatives, job associates, and neighbors to Christian ideals and truths.

Evangelism and outreach can and should play a major role through single adult weekday ministries. Again, since "everything we do involves outreach," programs can be planned to be enjoyable and also present the gospel.

Informal gospel concerts at parks, apartment units, or other neutral locations can be great evangelistic opportunities. Others also include self-help seminars that are based on gospel foundations, picnics with brief evangelistic messages presented, a singles festival or fair where tracts are distributed, or much more.

Outreach visitation can be tied to other weekly activities. This adds a spirit of variety and gets some singles involved in contacting others who otherwise might not do so.

Single adult ministries should involve missions in their weekday programming. This provides an avenue to help others with particular needs and builds character among Christian singles.

These mission projects could include Big Brother/Big Sister programs, leading Vacation Bible Schools or day camps, giving assistance at nursing homes, or helping a senior citizen with home repairs. Another could be serving an evening at the local mission center, preaching, singing, and giving personal testimonies. Each of these, and many more, gives singles a chance to become involved firsthand in missions. While helping others, they are helped. Most importantly, every mission project should always include an opportunity to share the plan of salvation with the persons to whom you are ministering.

Single adults love to eat! Many weekday activities can be centered around food. Be creative in your menu planning, meal locations, themes, and decorations. Make the occasion attractive so that people will want to come. Always have extra room and food for guests. Be prepared for the new person or persons who will come.

Entertainment of various kinds is a social need of adult singles. The church can provide wholesome Christian alternatives to what is regularly available to the single public. Many alternatives can be developed with creative thinking on the part of leadership.

Some suggestions include a talent extravaganza, a night at the movies where a good, entertaining movie can be rented and shown, Christian comedy programs, and more.

At every activity, name tags should be provided to aid in building fellowship and making it easier to open communication among those present.

Weekly ministry projects will only be as great an outreach tool as the single adult group dreams and desires it to be. Think big! Get the word out! Let singles of all ages know, whether they are members or not, that they are welcome.

At every activity take time for everyone to register, giving name, address, and other important information. This is a simple way to have needed material for follow-up with guests and new people. Member registration slips can simply be discarded. If both guests and members register, guests don't feel out of place or different.

It is vital that follow-up does take place. God entrusts the guests to the care of the single adult ministry to see that their primary spiritual need and other needs are met.

Take advantage of what you are probably already doing in weekday ministry. Use what you are doing as tools of evangelism, outreach, and proclaiming of the good news.

Single adults are "out there" by the millions waiting and wanting a place that is loving, caring, redemptive, accepting, and sincere. Be that place! Stand firm on God's Word, His principles, and His standards! Work hard! Plan well! Pray much! Know that outreach and revival will come!

21

Ethical Concerns

PAUL GRIFFIN JONES, II

Ethical concerns are a daily reality for the single adult. From early morning to late night, the single adult must face ethical crises and deal with moral and ethical issues about which he or she must make informed biblical decisions. The marketplace, the home, the social groups of society, and even the church all present the single adult with opportunities for ethical decision making.

Ethical Concern—A Basis for Spiritual Examination

The reality of human experience is that we all fail to keep the commitments that are so much a part of our daily experience. Personal integrity is often compromised on the altar of expediency. Propriety is often bartered at the door of social or group acceptance. Spiritual commitment is often replaced with personal concern and self-interest. The nature of the human experience is that of selective compromise and selfish decision making.

The realization that the human experience has caused us to deviate from and significantly alter our spiritual commitment is a basis for spiritual self-examination which can give rise to personal revival. The presence of the Holy Spirit of God in one's life causes an examination from time to time of the direction and basic commitments that propel us through life's pilgrimage. The opportunity to reexamine ethical and moral concerns will give the growing Christian an opportunity to initiate a closer spiritual walk and thus revival in his life.

A concern about personal morality and ethical living is, in fact, a true basis for revival and spiritual growth. The recognition of past failure and ethical impropriety can cause one to recommit both time and energy to a deeper spiritual pilgrimage. Ethical concerns, then, are a basis for spiritual examination which can lead to growth and maturity.

Ethical Concerns—A Basis for Social Involvement

Ethical concerns also provide a basis for propelling the Christian out into the world that is fragmented and fractious. The society in which the Christian lives is one that places strong emphasis upon a "me-istic" life-style. A Christian ethical concern for other persons and their social, cultural, racial, professional, as well as spiritual backgrounds, is a life-style that takes seriously the biblical mandate to take the gospel to all men and women everywhere.

The reality of prejudice, hatred, and social hurt, as well as the fact that so many persons find themselves without advocacy in a society that is increasingly becoming depersonalized, provide the individual Christian and the church an opportunity to carry the good news of the Savior who came to transform a world and its institutions. The single adult is in a unique place to provide both witness and challenge in the marketplace to those individuals who are involved within hurtful manipulations by social structures.

As the Christian single adult is given opportunity to address the hurt, the pain, and institutionalized problems of his or her society, the potential for revival is brought into sharper focus and the basis for revival, the improving of oneself so as to be able to address the hurts of others, is authenticated.

The single adult who has found means of applying his or her faith in the professional world (and therefore in the lives of colleagues and associates with whom he or she spends a large portion of the day) has perhaps discovered the basis of authentic witness. Witness is the living out of the life of Christ in a society that is increasingly hostile to the Christian faith and the ethical implications of obedience to that faith. A heightened social awareness will create within a single adult a deeper appreciation for and attention to the spiritual disciplines so necessary for the Christian life.

Ethical Concerns—A Basis for Authentic Life-style

It is perhaps axiomatic of the Christian faith that the true measure of one's commitment to Christ and to His church is actualized in authentic Christian life-style. The Christian faith is predicated upon the assumption that the believer in Jesus Christ will work out in his life a personalized expression of the life and ministry of Christ when He was on earth. Ethical and moral concerns which were so much a part of the day-by-day life of Jesus Christ must therefore be a consistent part of the contemporary Christian's confession.

The authentic Christian life-style is one that moves out of self and into an awareness of others. But it begins with a personal value system that demands integrity of living and loving that transcends that of the secular man. Matthew 25 gives an example of the authentic Christian life-style. It is concern for the hungry who have no food and the sick who have no one to care; it is the affirmation of those imprisoned without friends and the un-clothed without resources; and it is the outpouring of oneself to those who can provide nothing in return for our labor and ministry of love.

The authentic Christian life-style demands sexual purity, verbal integrity, visual consistency, and relational propriety that is unknown to the non-Christian world. It means surrendering one's desires and hopes and even needs to the higher good of the will of God.

The basis of the authentic Christian life-style is that of seeking to find and to do the will of God in human relations. This search or pilgrimage will cause a deepening of the awareness of the presence of God in one's life and, at the same time, an awareness of the reality of the power received from God through the Holy Spirit to live life at its fullest.

The authentic Christian life-style seeks Christ as its model in an attempt to minister to the hurts of persons and, at the same time, retain the basic integrity of Christian commitment. The life most open to the leadership of the Spirit of God is the life most prepared for revival and further spiritual challenge.

Ethical Concerns—A Basis for Revival

Must it not now be concluded that a concern about ethical and moral issues and about an authentic Christian life-style is the basis for any true revival? The affirmation of Scripture is that God enters the experience of those who are morally pure, ethically sound, and socially appropriate. If revival is predicated on the assumption of man's complete surrender to the will of God, then the measurable evidence of such surrender and commitment is seen in a Christian approach to ethical concerns.

A true revival will bring into sharp focus the social responsibility as well as the personal recommitment that is necessary for there to be a witness through ethical considerations. Likewise, a commitment to appropriate and biblical responses will ultimately bring the church to a point of total commitment to the will of God and thus to experience revival and renewal.

Again, we must examine the life of Christ to fully understand the role of ethical, moral, and social action on the Christian experience. Renewal within the covenant community began as Christ purged the Temple of those who would make it a "house of thieves." Concern about the morality and ethic of even the synagogue itself was a primary in the ministry of Christ. The life-style of the religious leaders was constantly being examined and weighed against the ethical teachings of Scripture, and too often the religious leaders were admonished for their lack of biblical justice and social responsibility.

Historically, when the church has accepted its responsibility to address those ethical and moral concerns that affect the lives of persons and the institutions of society, the great revivals of human history have begun. It would seem that it is impossible for there to be authentic spiritual revival without the church addressing the problem of its own integrity and witness and the structures of society which so easily harm the individuals who turn to it for help.

For a true revival to occur, there must be an addressing of the fundamental ethical concerns of human living. The single adult must be confronted, challenged, and convicted of the necessity for addressing these ethical concerns and for bearing witness to the grace of Christ which comes into a world whose ethic and morality has been compromised. Ethical concerns are, in fact, a basis for authentic revival.

22

Confrontation

RALPH E. HUNT

Rollen Stewart is the kind of Christian who seems to be the perfect stereotype of what nonbelievers term "fanatic." You say, "Who is Rollen Stewart?" You know him for sure; in fact, he is recognizable to millions. He is the wild-haired (actually it's a wig dyed orange) man with the John 3:16 T-shirt (now do you know Rollen?). He's been seen on Monday night football, on the PGA tour, at the superstars competition, even at the royal wedding of Prince Charles and Lady Di. It seems that every time the camera scans the crowd, there is Rollen, bobbing and waving, drawing attention to the message emblazoned on his chest. Stephen Olford met Stewart at the Western Open near Chicago and says he found him to be "an intelligent, quiet Christian who feels he has a clear call from God to witness in his unusual manner." Oh yes, when last seen, Rollen was single.

Most Christians I know cringe at the thought of such exaggerated "witnessing." They see it as demeaning the gospel and causing harm to the cause of Christ. Quite frankly, I must count myself as part of the group. We feel uncomfortable about the wild display. Yet I have a friend who had an opportunity to witness to a lost brother as they watched the Detroit Lions on television and saw a huge sign Rollen Stewart dropped over the balcony of the Silver Dome in Pontiac, Michigan, which read (you guessed it) "John 3:16." "What do those numbers mean?" the brother asked. "Let me tell you about it," replied my friend Tim.

Our friend Rollen has found a way to be a witness for Christ.

You may not agree with his methods, but then again, he might say, "Fine, what method do you use?"

The idea of taking the Bible off the shelf and witnessing to a friend or neighbor is as appealing as it is frightening. We don't want to come off as fanatical; yet at some point it is not enough just to live the Christian life. We must confront people with the gospel message. How do we motivate single adults and singles workers to take the gospel to the streets? See if this sounds familiar:

Carl, Betty, and Susan have just pulled into the parking lot of the apartment complex near the church.

"This guy's name is Bill Martin; he lives with Jim Wing in apartment 3-B," says Carl, eyeing the darkened window on the second floor.

"It doesn't look like he's home; maybe we should go to the next assignment," Susan adds, trying not to seem nervous.

"Well, he visited the church, and he said that he had questions about his relationship with God," Betty adds bravely. "I think we should knock on the door. He might be home."

Carl takes the lead and gets out of the car, followed by Betty and Susan. They walk up one flight and face the door of 3-B.

"I hear music," Susan whispers.

"Maybe they left the stereo on," Carl says as he tries to look through the peephole. "I do it all the time—you know, in case robbers comes, they think you're home."

"Well, does either one of you feel led to knock?" asks Betty. "I'm not feeling good about this situation."

"Betty!" Susan whispers, "you're leaning against the doorbell!

A light comes on, and Bill Martin opens the door and invites the three in. Forty minutes later, Bill invites Christ into his life.

What is the proper approach to witnessing? What role does the church play in the process of training and encouraging personal evangelism? How do we involve single adults in one-on-one witnessing?

First Things First

At the outset, let's be honest. Personal evangelism is one of the most difficult programs to maintain in any church. It never seems to get any easier. It is misunderstood (I know they'll let me out

111

in the middle of the K-Mart parking lot with a big bundle of gospel tracts!), confused (We already have a bumper sticker), and misrepresented (I don't have that spiritual gift). While possibly only 10 percent have "the gift," we all have "the Giver," and He says through the apostle Paul in 2 Timothy 4:5 to "do the work of an evangelist." What is that work? To lead others to Christ.

Where to Begin?

Southern Baptists have majored on evangelism from day 1. Today the emphasis is on both confrontational and relational or life-style evangelism. Some are opting for life-style evangelism at the expense of the confrontational approach. Robert Hamblin, director of evangelism for the Home Mission Board, believes this is a mistake. "I've tried it both ways. You win a lot more people with relationships than confrontation. But you win some through confrontation. Some relationships will never be developed. Some people will never be a part of an environment where I can form a relationship with them. There's no bad way to win a person to Christ."[1] I believe that we must be prepared to confront our friends and neighbors with the gospel when the moment arises. It is always best to win a trusted friend because the relationships grow and continue.

A Few Statistics

Win Arn asked 8,000 church members this question: "Why are most people in your church part of your church?" Walk-ins, program, pastor, special need, visitation, crusade, and Sunday School accounted for a total of 10 to 30 percent. Significantly, friends and relatives account for 70 to 90 percent.[2] He went on to say that each church member has an average of 8.4 unchurched friends or relatives who are candidates for the gospel.

Sterling Huston of the Billy Graham Evangelistic Association reports that "75 percent of all who come forward at our crusades were brought by a friend or family member, and 80 to 90 percent of the completely unchurched who make commitments came because someone they knew had done the sowing and watering."[3]

It is clear that lasting decisions come from cultivated prospects. So what is the role of confrontation in the process of someone

112

coming to Christ? Simply stated: Someone has to train the friends and relatives to witness!

First-Century Evangelism

We look to Scripture to find the proper balance. Acts 2:40-47 is a handbook for church growth and evangelism. First there is the call from the pulpit to respond to Jesus Christ. "Be saved from the perverse generation" (v. 40 *b*). Next we read of training to reproduce their life in others (v. 42) and a sacrifice of time and resources for the gospel (v. 45) and the resultant outreach because they found "favor with *all* the people" (v. 47, author's italics). The point is that the Word was preached and many were saved. The people were taught, and they met the needs (made new friends) of others. The result was many persons for the kingdom. They won the favor of all the people (they were *trusted* by their friends, neighbors, and relatives). Jesus had made a recognizable difference in their lives, and they evidently knew how to share Christ one-on-one. How were they taught to witness? We can only speculate, but they must have had skills in personal evangelism.

Twentieth-Century Model

As we look at the role of the single adult in the outreach of the church, could it be that they are indeed a vital part of the process? Yes! May I suggest the following?

Every church needs to establish an on-going evangelism training program. It is best to offer a smorgasbord approach, offering different training for different levels of commitment. Here are a few suggestions.

1. *Three-Week Approach to Witnessing Course.* Offer a forty-five-minute class prior to your weekly visitation. Recruit several leaders to take "silent witnesses" on visitation for each of the three weeks. Give practical instruction on "How to Break the Ice," "Giving Your Personal Testimony," "Using a Witnessing Booklet to Share Christ." Make materials available, and be sure to have a report session with refreshments.

2. *Use the TELL Machine* (available from the Home Mission Board, SBC). Most associations and many churches have one of these little machines. You can offer an ongoing class at the

Church Training hour. The cassettes can be used in a variety of ways—from one week to several.

3. *Lay Evangelism School.* Schedule a LES session for your church. It involves people, brightens awareness of the need for outreach, and trains scores of new witnesses for Christ.

4. *Continuing Witness Training.* Many singles love the CWT process because it is really a first-step discipleship course that emphasizes witnessing skills. I believe this is the best approach to use with singles. You can receive training by attending a CWT national seminar in your area. To find out about the details, contact your state Baptist convention evangelism office.

Why Are Some So Successful in Witnessing and Others Are Not?

There is a young woman in our church called Bo. She leads so many people to Christ that it is amazing. How does she do it? Why is she so successful? Two reasons: First, she knows *how* to share the gospel; second, she *shares* it. We are so afraid of rejection that we forget what good news we really have in our possession! Confrontation makes us feel uncomfortable, so we tend to avoid it. But we must keep things in perspective. The battle we fight is not so much against time pressures, public opinion, and apathy. It is against the unseen powers of darkness (Eph. 6:12). The tension we feel is a result of the spiritual warfare in which we are involved, not of "putting someone on the spot." We need to expect those moments and work through them. Those who do are able to lead people to Christ. Those who do not may share their faith but rarely have the joy of praying with a new believer to invite Christ into his or her life.

Where Do We Begin?

Pray, plan, study, train—but above all, begin. Let me share a true story in closing:

During my senior year of college, I decided that it was time for me to develop some skills in personal evangelism. My wife and I attended a Lay Institute for Evangelism course. It was wonderful to learn how to pray for lost people and to share the gospel in a straightforward manner. One morning in one of the sessions, we were asked to use the "Four Spiritual Laws" booklet and read

114

it to the person seated next to us. I did the best I could, and the man even went through the prayer section. After we finished, the instructor asked if anyone had prayed the prayer, inviting Christ into their life for the first time. My new friend raised his hand! As we closed in prayer, we asked the Lord to give us opportunities to share Christ that week. I prayed, knowing that I was attending a Christian college, was married to a wonderful Christian woman, and worked at a large Christian publishing company. I figured that as long as I didn't have to stop for gas on the way to work, I probably wouldn't even meet a nonbeliever.

The next day was routine. Morning classes, chapel, lunch, then off to work (with a full tank!). I put in a good afternoon at work, talking with pastors on the phone and finishing my calls around 9:00 PM. I stood to leave and was taping a beautiful color photo I had clipped from *Decision* magazine on my wall just as the night watchman walked into the room.

"Hello."

"Hello, Mike," I said, somewhat unnerved by the tingling sensation going up and down my spine.

"What's that?" Mike said, gesturing with a nod of his head toward the photo.

"Oh, that . . . that's, uh . . . you know, about evangelism and things like that."

"Evangelism, huh?" he said, staring at the photo. "You know, I've always wanted to know more about that."

"Really?" I said with a shuffle. "Maybe we could talk about it sometime."

As I opened my desk drawer to put my pencil in the tray, I spotted a Four Laws booklet and picked it up. Mike and I stood looking at the little gold booklet without saying anything.

"What's that?"

"The uh, four, uh, spiritual laws," I said in a voice that seemed to be an octave higher than normal. "Ever hear of it?"

"No, but I'd really like to."

Ten minutes later, Mike and I were on our knees and he was inviting Jesus Christ into his life as Savior and Lord. As we got up off our knees, Mike said something that I'll never forget.

"Why hasn't anyone ever told me this before?"

"I don't know, Mike . . . maybe they thought you weren't interested."

Mike's job was to guard Sunday School literature and Bibles. But nobody had ever taken the time to confront him with the gospel, the good news of Jesus Christ. He thought it was great news. So do I. Oh yes, Mike was single and engaged to be married. The first thing he did was pick up the phone and call his fiancée to tell her of his decision.

Let's equip our single adults to confront their world with the good news.

---

1. Tim Stafford, "Evangelism: The New Wave Is a Tidal Wave," *Christianity Today*, May 18, 1984, p. 65.
2. Win Arn, "Making Visitation Fruitful," *Eternity*, June 1983, p. 45.
3. *Christianity Today*, p. 43.

23

Preaching

CHARLES B. BAKER

Preparing for and preaching to single adults is exactly like preaching to anyone else except for remembering that they are single. That is an oversimplified statement, but it involves a great deal of truth.

Single adults have a great capacity to be strongly relationship oriented. With this in mind, sermons that seem to gain their attention and respect are those that apply the truths of the Bible to relationship living. They are not as interested in proving the existence of God through the scientific laboratories as they are experiencing a loving God in the living relationships of everyday life.

Single adults seem to respond with a great deal of attention to presentation of the life of Jesus Christ. They are interested in how He lived in relationship to His friends, the power structure of His day, the cultural barriers, and the political system. As a sermon retraces the footsteps of Jesus into all the arenas of life, singles can identify. They need to know that the single of singles, Jesus Christ, did encounter every type of relationship that they can expect to be a part of. As they see Him come alive in the realities of the same struggles that they themselves face, they respond. Singles, then, seem to respond more to the messages that tell them how to relate to life and life's circumstances.

With this relationship orientation to life, when one is preaching through the letters of Paul and John and Peter, biblical background information makes a difference. Where was Paul when he was writing to the Philippians? What kind of situation did he find himself in where he had the right to say: "Rejoice in the Lord always; again I will say, rejoice!" (Phil. 4:4). When the single listener hears that Paul is writing from a jail cell and still giving instructions about being positive, he has a deeper appreciation for the author's right to give such an instruction.

Singles face many problems, but constructive preaching puts opportunities before them rather than discouraging them by reiterating problems. Focus on the positive aspects of singleness such as the possible freedom from spouse and children that would open up opportunities for travel involvement in missions and broad varied relationships. This is the kind of freedom that can allow the single to live the Christian life the way Jesus did in ministry and servanthood. Of course, this is the goal of every Christian, but the single has some real advantages in this quest.

Singles have an opportunity to demonstrate Christ's love to the community as they care for each other—doing things that would normally be taken care of by other members of a family unit. For singles who are hurting because of loss of a loved one through death or divorce, nothing can help more in the healing process than a redemptive ministry to someone else. Preaching can keep this challenge before them, encouraging them to look beyond their own pain to others in need.

The delivery of the sermon itself should indicate openness. Pulpits can be a help or a hindrance in communicating. When one senses from the hearer's standpoint that the speaker is separated from him, the pulpit may be standing in the way of good communication. Sometimes it is better to remove the pulpit or to walk around to the side. The closer the preacher is to the audience in physical and attitudinal stance, the better the message is received as being authentic. The subject of the sermon should be relevant. An up-to-date application is needed in every message. Singles are living in a real world with real opportunities and difficulties.

The diverse interest of a congregation, including singles, is amazing. In the audience may be everyone from the young singles by choice to the grandmother single who has recently lost a husband of many years. Yet they all have common needs. All get lonely, feel a sense of desperation, face daily problems, seek love and laughter, and need a growing relationship with Jesus Christ.

Keep the sermon brief. Preach about Jesus Christ in about twenty minutes or less. The sermon might well be confined to one topic.

Consider opening a time at the end of a sermon for questions. This can be a great time of clarification and it also develops a trust level with the audience and helps them know that there is a genuine concern to listen and present Jesus in such a way that the needs of their lives are met. Have an excellent beginning and ending. Many a sermon has gotten off to a great start and continued to progress far too long. Know how you are going to bring the sermon to a conclusion.

Ask for a response. Expect a response! When Jesus Christ is presented as the One who can meet needs, people will respond. Many decisions can be made without one's ever coming forward. Always keep this in mind. In the concluding remarks, call attention to the fact that some decisions need to be made in the pews and carried directly out into the workaday world. Yet there are other decisions that will need the support of the whole church family. Give persons the opportunity to step forward and celebrate how God has spoken to them.

Most of all, be convinced and excited about your sermon. Be convinced that it is needed and that it can help. Keep it positive. Remember, the Father has given us the privilege of delivering good news to a hurting world—not bad news. Singles will respond to the positive loving presentation of the Scripture and its application to their lives.

24

Bible Study

DAVID RODDY

Bible Fellowships (the Sunday School class and the apartment Bible study) can be the creative answer to reaching the expanding single adult population of America, probably the most neglected and most difficult segment of society to reach with the gospel of Jesus Christ. Churches that will reach single adults must set a priority for reaching and teaching them through *effective* Bible fellowships because the evangelism of the 80s goes much further than simply making a "decision," signing a decision statement, praying a prayer, or going forward in a worship service. Making decisions for Christ is an essential part of true evangelism, but the new evangelism is the total work of obeying the imperative verb to "make disciples" through friendship or relational evangelism. The evangelistic goal is nothing less than making disciples for Jesus Christ.

What are some essentials in evangelizing single adults?

Confidence in God's Word

The purpose of the Bible is to bring God and human together in living and loving fellowship. Because the Bible is God's Word dealing with life with God, life now, and life hereafter, single adults are very open and receptive to the Bible.

God has designed His Word with authority to effect change in lives. "The word of God is living and active" (Heb. 4:12), wrote the author of Hebrews. Peter described its power when he wrote, "born again . . . through the living and abiding word of God" (1 Pet. 1:23). Jesus on several occasions said, "It is written," and He used the written Word as the basis for His authority. Effective Bible teaching is centered in God's Word with the teacher having confident trust in the power and authority of that Word to effect changes in the lives of listeners (Isa. 55:11).

The Bible has a central place in every fellowship session. Pupils are taught to bring their Bibles and use them. Extra Bibles are available for those without. As the Bibles are opened and read, the Holy Spirit teaches and illuminates the mind of the reader. Usage of modern translations is encouraged.

Understanding Single Adults

Singles are constantly searching. They look first for meaningful relationships, for someone they can call a friend. They are looking for answers to the crises of living of today's world. They see chaotic world conditions, instability with few roots, meaningless center point for life, breakdown of homelife, unfulfillment in a vocation, confusion of moral standards, and the unfulfillment of status. They are seeking stability and direction. They hunger for love in an intensely cold and nonpersonal world. They long for reality, but understanding where it is and when it comes is the key problem. To the single mind, reality is often thought of as being in status or circumstance—vocational success, money, marriage, popularity, things, or position. The temptation is to postpone reality by living in a "when . . . then" ("When certain things happen, then I will feel complete, whole, and fulfilled") kind of unreal world. Bruce Larson shares this thought.

> The neighborhood bar is possibly the best counterfeit there is to the fellowship Christ wants to give His church. It's an invitation, dispensing liquor instead of grace, escape rather than reality, but it is permissive, accepting an inclusive fellowship. The bar flourishes not because most people are alcoholics, but because God has put in the heart the desire to know and be known, to love and be loved, and so many seek a counterfeit at the price of a few beers.[1]

Are we, the church, capable of reaching out to these singles with authentic love and care? Bible fellowships can provide the answer.

The Surrounding Influence in a Bible Fellowship

The quality of group fellowship is the factor most single adults look for first as strangers in a new group: "That was a warm, caring class! Bible study today was most meaningful!" "That was a friendly class" or "The class really did welcome me!" It is important to make our classes reaching out and caring communities. Single adults are drawn to our Bible fellowships more often by the warmth of relationships than by the brilliance of the Bible exposition.

If the class attitude is cold, distant, uncaring, self-centered, "a pity party," apathetic, and implosive, you can rest assured, Bible study in such a fellowship will repel non-Christian single adults.

A genuine caring fellowship will find greeters at the door, teachers and class officers mingling with the pupils and attending to visitors, visitors having someone to talk with and sit with, visitors accompanied to worship or to a meal after church, visitors offered a Bible, visitors properly introduced and applauded during class, and visitors contacted during the week or accompanied by fellowship members to socials, apartment Bible studies, and other social events of the class. Few single adults would rebel against membership in such a dynamic caring group.

The Sunday Bible Fellowship

Bible lessons carry many themes and titles. No matter what the subject, an evangelistic thrust can be a part of every lesson plan. Teachers should look and pray for an evangelistic direction of the lesson. An evangelistic response can be called for.

Bible study emphasizes the Christian position of being a friend to the non-Christian world in order to bring about reconciliation between God and man. It teaches and motivates the Christian to be a witness to his world of influence.

Bible study shows the many opportunities and approaches that are available to the Christian for witnessing. In the New Testament, multitudes of Christians fled the tragic persecutions in Jerusalem, but they went everywhere sharing their faith. The Bible illustrates the unlimited potential in personal witnessing.

Bible study creates a concern for lost persons. The lostness of people not knowing Christ is made real through Bible study, and Christians are placed under the responsibility of sharing Christ in a personal witness.

It is in Bible study that the love of Christ for all persons is revealed. It is in Bible study that concern for the single adults of a city is generated. It is in Bible study that Christians discover they are to function in the world as God's "salt," "light," and "leaven." It is through Bible study that single adults are challenged to be God's unique task force in the world. Apart from the

Bible study, few single adults ever become involved in meeting human need in the name of Christ.

The Sunday morning Bible fellowship is the Christian single adult's most meaningful experience. The entire experience can radiate with an evangelistic thrust.

Apartment Bible Fellowships

Conducting Bible fellowships in the apartment complexes where the vast majority of single adults live is one of the best strategies available for reaching single adults. House churches were the norm in the early church (Acts 2:46; 5:42; 20:20; Col. 4:15). Single adults want to *see* the gospel and *feel* the impact of the gospel. The apartment Bible fellowship approach to evangelizing is basic relational evangelism. What better place for single adults to be "salt," "light," and "leaven" than in the people–filled areas of apartment complexes. When a Bible study fellowship is started by a Christian single in an apartment complex, he reaches out to those nearest him, who see his life daily exposed, who feel his continuing caring love, and who sense God's channel of grace for searching hearts. Many single adults have been won to faith in Jesus Christ because a caring and loving Christian single began reaching out to those in his world who live nearest him, through the beginning of a small Bible study fellowship in apartment complexes.

This type of evangelism releases hundreds of single adults to new levels of responsibility in leadership. It is important that the apartment Bible fellowships be an extension or a part of the outreach ministry of the single adult Bible fellowship of the local church. This will keep the apartment fellowship strong and coordinated; it will prevent the fellowship from developing into divisive cells of disorder, fanaticism, immorality, or division.

Leadership should be trained in evangelistic Bible study. Such training should teach the leadership how to avoid pet denominational doctrine, how to explain "churchy" language strange to the non-Christian, how to establish growing relationships with neighbors, how to be available to the hurting, confused, and lonely, how to point the non-Christian single to basic passages of Scripture that relate to an evangelistic response, and, above all, how to share what Jesus Christ means to life.

Joan Fox is a young twenty-eight-year-old Christian single with a deep commitment to reaching her apartment complex with an evangelistic Bible fellowship. She prayed and waited for God to engineer positive circumstances. One Saturday afternoon, she saw thirty to forty single adults lounging around the apartment pool. Her vision led to the creative idea of preparing a salad buffet and inviting the crowd to a free refreshment break. She hurried off to the store, purchasing tasty ingredients. After the preparation, she walked out her apartment door and publicly announced, "Free food!" Single adults seem to always be hungry, so the response was very positive. From the initial response, several new friendships were started. In one month, she was able to begin a Saturday morning Bible reading and sharing fellowship. From three to now ten, with four non-Christians attending, this Bible fellowship is reaching single adults.

Bible Fellowship "Beachheads"

Single adults can be led to establish "beachheads" in their places of business. A "beachhead" is a miniprayer/sharing/Bible reading time lasting no longer than fifteen minutes conducted at work.

Two single architects working in the same building decided they wanted to take fifteen minutes of their thirty-minute lunch break to spend in reading some verses of Scripture, sharing what Christ was doing in their lives, and praying. They did not promote their meeting, but after two months, they were joined by a third person; and now, six months later, of the twelve persons in their "beachhead," nine are single.

Most single adults have great opportunities for witnessing and ministry build into their life-styles. The gospel of Christ must go into the marketplaces of life; and what better way with a quiet, nonpublicized time of Bible sharing during work break or lunch break.

Conclusion

Evangelizing single adults should be the church's priority of the 1980s if it expects to move out to the growing edge. This is not only the greatest but the most responsive mission field in the world today. The churches who are winning single adults to

Christ have strong Bible teaching fellowships. The time to reach and teach single adults is now. Prioritize your Bible fellowship to reach out to single adults.

1. Bruce Larson, *Dare to Live Now* (Grand Rapids: Zondervan Publishing House, 1965), p. 110.

25

Campus Ministries

LARRY GOLDEN

The university campus is a unique community. At first glance, you see an unreal world that is a strange mixture of society. Not being familiar with this academic community while trying to find a handle for ministry can be frustrating. But there is a common factor that relates ministry on the college campus to ministry in any environment, no matter how unique that environment may be.

A second glance at the university community reveals the common factor: people with needs. Stand on any corner of any campus and you see the students, faculty, and staff. These people make the sterile, unreal academic world into a very real community, a community with the same needs that we Christians discover to be common among everyone.

The Student Resource

Revival through campus ministry is synonymous with students reaching students. Each year students arrive on campus with a readiness for God. They are often the untapped resource of revival. These students stand with extension cord in hand waiting to be shown where to plug in their lives for their Lord.

These students come with a variety of gifts. Some of these gifts are already developed. Other students simply need the time and space to bloom. In both cases, these students have the time and willingness to be ministers. The church only needs to be creative in assimilating these students into the church's structure for revival.

The church that is providing opportunities for student involvement is scheduling its structure to meet the needs of the student. The semester or quarter cycles of the college calendar may not fit well with the thirteen-week quarter system that we are used to in our churches. The starting and stopping times of the college calendar may not always coincide with the normal church schedule. Events such as midterms, finals, and homecoming are very important considerations when planning events related to revival.

All of the resources students bring with them to school have potential application for revival. Some of these gifts are more obvious and traditional than others. A student with musical ability may be easier to locate and use than a student with communication skills in writing. But both skills can be important to an evangelistic event.

Planning and managing are the keys to the effective use of the student resources. Due to the time space of the school year, involving students is usually a very intense task. The hard work becomes worth the effort when you see these students growing in discipleship and their enthusiasm spreading to other areas of church life.

The Campus as Recipient for Revival

Effective revival goes beyond the four walls of the church. The college students, faculty, and staff who are members of your church are the vehicles for taking revival to the campus. Organizing and training these groups become an important part of the revival process.

Revival is both an event and a process. The process leads to a specific evangelistic event. The process also helps sustain the harvest of the event. If revival is to be lasting, then it is important that your students, faculty, and staff be organized and trained.

Training activities should include opportunities for personal witness training. Continual Witnessing Training, Friendship Evangelism Seminars, Share Seminars, WIN schools, and EvangeLife Seminars should be part of the process. Other training in discipleship should include MasterLife, *The Survival Kit for New*

Christians, and other courses that enhance personal spiritual growth. Special seminars should include training in how to lead Bible studies and discussion groups as well as in how to relate specific academic areas to the gospel.

Organizing your students, faculty, and staff means helping them set up Bible studies and discussion times on campus. This may mean scheduling breakfasts or luncheons for faculty and staff or late night dorm discussion groups for the students. Other possibilities might include arranging luncheons around topics of broad social interest such as world hunger. The organizing and training provides opportunities for the gospel to be presented to those who would not walk into a church building.

The Baptist Student Union Resource

When making plans to take revival beyond your church's walls, do not overlook the strategic place of the local Baptist Student Union. The Baptist Student Union has long been at work providing effective ways to bring about revival on campus. Many times the best approach for outreach on campus may be found working through the structure that the Baptist Student Union has already built. If this is not the case, the Baptist Student Union can serve as a resource to help the church build its own structure.

The local church and the Baptist Student Union can plan together for effective outreach. There is always a greater need for sharing the good news on the campus than any one church or other campus ministry group can manage.

The Baptist Student Union can also help the local church by providing the types of training mentioned in the previous section. At times the Baptist Student Union can provide students as a resource for revival. Through a Baptist Student Union's revival team ministry, students might help lead in a revival. These students would use their gifts by actually preaching, leading music, and organizing publicity for the revival.

Churches in Noncollege Communities

Even if your church is not located in a college town, you still have a stake in helping bring about revival through campus ministries. Every church usually has at least one student who is away at college. Your church has a definite ministry to perform for that student.

Continuing the process of revival in students' lives after they are attending college is important in the discipleship of your Christian student. It is also essential to the evangelization of that student who is not a believer. Knowing that love and caring transcend geographical space will speak to a student away from home. Students are helped by the anchor of home and knowing that there are those who remember them as more than just a number.

Letters and phone calls of encouragement can continue to provide growth opportunities for your Christian student and witnessing encounters for your nonbelieving student. When possible, visiting your student on campus can be most effective.

Churches can also provide support for evangelistic emphases that take place on campuses. As mentioned earlier, the Baptist Student Union already has ongoing programs as well as planned special events that relate to evangelism on campus. At the same time, on any campus, there is more that needs to be done than there are resources. Your church might help this situation by staying alert to the needs and programs of the Baptist Student Union. Becoming a partner in campus ministry with the Baptist Student Union can make the difference between the total campus hearing or not hearing the gospel.

Actions for Revival

It has already been mentioned that training and organizing students, faculty, and staff are important to the revival process. Listed below are some possible activities to enhance revival through campus ministries. Of course, not all activities work equally well in all situations. Most of all, the list is meant to be an idea starter for your particular ministry. As you read these actions, have a pen in hand to jot down those specific ideas that come to mind that you can apply to your particular situation.

1. Student, faculty, and staff visitation teams.
2. Discussion groups starting four weeks before the revival event centering around the person of Jesus Christ.
3. Prerevival rally on campus.

4. Evangelism training targeted to the students, faculty, and staff.

5. Luncheons for faculty and staff.

6. Publish the Christian testimonies of faculty, students, and staff in the campus paper.

7. Plan discussion times with students, faculty, and staff that relate to living the Christian life on campus.

8. Dorm rap sessions after revival services.

9. Plan use of student talent during the revival services.

10. Develop a committee of students to direct the student emphasis portion of the revival.

11. Use students from another church or from the Baptist Student Union to lead the revival.

12. Sponsor a student revival team at a mission chapel.

13. Use students to contact all university students through a telephone bank.

14. Use student music and drama teams to publicize the revival on campus and in the community.

15. Organize students, faculty, and staff prayer meetings.

The Campus Mission Field

The unique characteristics of the campus community make it a very concentrated mission field. Revival through campus ministry means mobilizing student, faculty, and staff to meet the needs of this community. The needs are great. The stakes are high.

Leaders are training for the future. They will lead the world into the twenty-first century and beyond. Will these leaders have the opportunity to respond to the gospel of Jesus Christ? The challenge is ours.

26

Community Missions

H. PAUL ROYAL

While He was here among us in flesh and blood, Jesus showed us what it means to be a servant. "For I gave you an example that you also should do as I did to you" (John 13:15), He said. Perhaps it was the words He used to describe servanthood that caused so many to politely reject His serving example—words like *last, least, suffering, humility.* These are the tough words, and the task of serving people who are in need is a tough task.

It is unfortunate that in many of our churches, we have effectively removed the influence of believers from sinners. Gayle E. Erwin declared, "Everywhere, Christian ghettos are springing up. The light is hidden under church pews rather than shining openly. We stand away from the sinner as he sweeps helplessly to this doom and safely advise him not to sweep helplessly to his doom."[1]

In a message to the members of Park Cities Baptist Church in Dallas, Texas, Dr. E. V. Hill, one of America's great black preachers, said that it is not a matter of there being no white people visible in the ghettos. He assured us that there were white policemen, white garbage collectors, white teachers, white drug pushers, white prostitutes, white insurance salesmen . . . the tragedy is, he said, that there are no recognized white Christians there.

In Dallas, as in other cities, the middle and upper classes—and their churches—have fled the growing urbanization by moving to the suburbs. People commute to their work and their routes may be arranged so that they go for days without seeing a poor person or one in whom great need is recognizable. Inner-city institutions have been left to dominate the lives of the poor by controlling everything from their housing to medical system, to food stamps, to welfare checks, to criminal and educational systems. And the Christian influence is hardly felt at all. Tragic!

The Bible is filled with instructions as to how God's children are to relate to the poor. Over one thousand verses record God's promising, describing, and commanding assistance to those who are in need. In the Old Testament, field owners were not allowed

129

to harvest fields all the way to the edges, and owners of vineyards were told not to harvest all the grapes from the vines. The grain and the grapes were to be left for the "poor and for the sojourners among you" (Lev. 19:9-10, RSV).

The method used in the Old Testament is hardly appropriate for twentieth-century believers. But the task is the same. Community missions speaks to how to go about that task on a local level.

Someone has said that the only irresistible Christian witness results when a Christian does a person with a great need a good deed in the name and Spirit of Christ. There is a close correlation, I believe, between life-style evangelism and community missions. And single adults are tremendous resources for both.

The direction of my personal ministry was radically altered by a statement made by Elton Trueblood. He said, "The current idea is that the pastor is one who has a program, and the people exist to support his ministry; the New Testament idea is that the people have a program and the pastor exists to support them."[2]

To discover what the program ideas are of the single adults I serve, I occasionally invite a dozen or more over for dinner and a brainstorming session. They always amaze me with individual abilities, potential, and creativity. The most widely accepted ideas and programs used in our ministry were initiated by one or more of the singles. One of the single adults came to me almost two years ago. She said, "Paul, I feel that most of what we do in the singles ministry here is for us, for each other. We do not really reach out to other people very much. Would you host a think tank to consider community missions as an optional opportunity for involvement for members of our group?"

The interest the singles showed in this brainstorming session amazed me. Three weeks later, we brought together all the singles departments for a Bible study on caring for people in need. Harv Oostdyk, founder of STEP Foundation, shared with the group strategies to elevate people and ideas for meeting the needs of the poor. Nearly five hundred of the singles signed up that day to begin a sustained ministry to the indigent through community missions.

Since then the entire church has adopted the strategies, and we are the lead church in the Rhoads Terrace section of Dallas. It is in South Dallas, hidden just beyond one of the expressways that can carry us quickly past the area without our ever seeing the housing project that is worse than most you would find in other major cities.

The STEP Council for our church, comprised of five single adults, accepted three premises for developing strategies for helping the impoverished folks in South Dallas.

Premise 1

We must recognize that the church needs to employ new and different strategies to help the urban poor in America. The church's programs to help the poor are still rooted in the past, but our society has changed. Automobiles have fostered the creation of suburbia, which geographically isolated the poor from the more wealthy. Many churches follow their worshipers out of the inner city. They had previously had great impact on needy families. Governmental institutions were created in time to fill the void. They now dominate the lives of the poor.

Premise 2

We must understand that a blueprint to solve the tangled problems of the poor must be complex. Do not be frustrated if you don't grasp it at first. You would have trouble understanding the plans for a skyscraper at once. The federal government has spent billions for years and has been largely unable to reverse the cycle of poverty. Helping the poor is not an easy undertaking.

Premise 3

We must be careful to include the "together" people of the target neighborhood in all aspects of the plan. Sometimes we forget that there are some solid citizens living in our ghettos. No one knows these areas better than the civic-minded folks, many of them Christians, who have wept over the problems for years.

A decision was made to begin our work in the elementary school and the community recreation center that served the Rhoads Terrace area. A Friendship Committee made up of three people from our church was formed to relate to many of the institutional leaders there: the school principal, the teachers, the director of the housing project, the directors of the community recreation center.

The Friendship Committee would approach the person it was assigned to befriend simply by introducing themselves and asking how they could be helpful. As expected, this approach was viewed with suspicion and even some resentment by the institutional leaders. "What do you want to do? Tell us how to do our jobs? Why are you so concerned about what's happening down here?"

Some dealt with the offer more creatively. When the principal of the school was first approached, he assured the Friendship Committee that he could really use their help. "We need someone to police the toilets." He thought, *That will let me know if they are for real.* They were for real. And with each visit of his newfound friend, he shared more and more of his dreams and frustrations. His school had a serious attendance problem, and the teacher turnover was tremendous. Supported by Friendship Teams for himself and most of his teaching staff, he led his school from the highest rate of absenteeism to the best attendance record in the Dallas Independent School District within a two-year period.

Many things contributed to this transformation. Tutors were enlisted to give special attention to the students who needed it. Incentives were offered to encourage attendance. The class who won a six-week contest offering a free "feast" at a nearby Mac-Donalds had a 99.6 percent attendance record. That was up from about 60 percent.

The school building was old and in poor repair. The principal asked his Friendship Committee for help in painting a "few murals" on the wall. A team of artists, graphics experts, and architects were pulled together from our singles group. The chairman of that action group said, "To put a few murals on the wall would be like offering a Band-aid to a person who needed open heart surgery."

The group began to dream and visualize what the building could look like. After several weeks, they had developed a comprehensive plan that was ultimately enthusiastically endorsed by the school administration. As a result of their working together, the Thompson Elementary School has undergone a transformation that is truly miraculous. Teachers now request to be transferred to that school rather than from it. The community is proud of it. There is now a PTA that proudly looks for ways to support *their* school.

Encouraged by the responsibility and consistency shown in the school, the president of the Dallas Housing Authority accepted the offer of his Friendship Committee to attempt to reroof the entire Rhoads Terrace Housing Project. Over five hundred volunteers showed up on work day. While the entire project was not completed, an incredible amount of work was accomplished.

Bible studies, camping trips, sporting events, and other activities provide our ministry teams with the opportunity and right to share their faith with a lot of people who had been previously overlooked.

Single adults are eager to be a vital part of the church and its ministries. They are capable, creative, willing, and available. They need to be involved in the lives of other people. They are responsive to things that are spiritual. There is no better resource for evangelism, for revival, for community missions than single adults. And they really want and need to receive the blessings that come from a vital and active relationship with Jesus Christ.

---

1. Gayle D. Erwin, *The Jesus Style* (Palm Springs, California: Ronald N. Hayes Pub., Inc.), p. 67.

2. Elton Trueblood, *The Incendiary Fellowship* (New York: Harper & Row, 1965), p. 53.

27

Special Events

BILL MYERS

In order to reach the single adult community, we must provide attractive events to bring them to our churches. Sometimes we must be away from the church to interest them. Some events and special activities are listed below.

Concerts

Some concerts may be free, others at a ticket cost. In enlisting concert personnel, be sure to have a definite understanding as to fees, love offerings, or honorariums. Most well-known artists will have you sign a contract stating the terms of the concert. Be careful not to have concerts too often.

If you have a pay concert, plan a budget including cost of the artist, accompanists, travel, lodging, food, any cost of auditorium (if not held at the church), printing of numbered tickets, publicity, and any miscellaneous expenses. Then determine your potential audience. From these two figures, you are able to determine the cost of the tickets.

Be sure to use printed numbered tickets for sales assignment purposes. Tickets can be distributed through Christian and other book stores, ticket outlets, and by church and Sunday School personnel. Assign tickets by numbers so you will know at all times where your tickets are and so they can be accounted for at the end of the sales.

Don't be afraid to use paid publicity such as radio and newspaper. Television ads are good but very expensive. Of course, don't overlook traditional publicity such as posters, fliers, and word of mouth of church members. Mail fliers and posters to all churches in the city. Posters should be placed in as many apartment clubhouses or bulletin boards where single adults live as possible.

A concert organization should include a steering committee composed of the chairpersons of these committees: publicity, ticket printing (and sales for paid concert), welcome and ushers, stage (lighting, sound, etc.), hospitality, fellowship (if any is planned before or after the concert), and any other needed committee. Remember, the more people involved, the better.

An important factor is to have your singles wear name tags and to meet (get acquainted with) concert attendees. During the concert, maybe during the break, be sure to have an effective presentation of your single adult ministry. A brief slide presentation is a good possibility. Be very imaginative at this point.

Also, if you plan to do another concert, be sure to have the date and personnel enlisted so you can announce it. You might even have the tickets for sale.

Friday Evening Programs

Friday Nite Live—Our church has a nonprofit restaurant called the 4th Street Inn. We have use of the restaurant on Friday evenings. It is open for singles to come and eat at cost. When there is live entertainment, a cover charge of one dollar helps defray entertainment honorarium. Our singles mingle with prospects to enlist them in the single adult ministry. A volunteer manager heads the food and server volunteers. He is responsible for the entertainment also. A number of these prospects are enlisted in our single adult ministry.

Fabulous Fridays—My former single adult ministry had Friday night programs. A committee of singles planned, promoted, and executed the total program. At first we used every Friday night but found that it was hard to maintain quality that frequently. A twice-a-month schedule was then adopted. For budgetary reasons, qualified persons in the church and community were used as speakers and/or musicians most of the time. Church members were not paid but asked to serve as a part of their Christian service. Registration and name tags helped to identify prospects. An important feature of the Fabulous Fridays was an informal fellowship following the program. Most of the programs were held at the church to ensure that the prospects became acquainted with the church.

Friday Night Bible Studies—These can be sponsored by a Sunday School class or individual singles. Teachers must be church approved. The most effective way of outreach is to select an individual who lives in an apartment complex where many singles live and ask that person to schedule the club room for a period of Friday evenings for a Bible study. Appropriate announcements should be placed on the apartment bulletin boards and in the laundry areas. The program could include a covered dish supper, a time of fellowship and getting acquainted, and Bible study. The better the Bible teacher (single or married), the easier it will be to reach and keep prospects. The purpose of the Friday night Bible study is to reach the prospect, acquaint him with your singles, guide him to faith in Jesus Christ, and enlist him in the church. Remember the primary purpose of your Bible study is to become a self-serving group.

Direct Mail

Professional mailing companies can provide areas (and in some cases lists) of single adults. Attractive brochures or other effective materials can be mailed to single adults. Professional mailers say that some kind of response should be asked for. This is very expensive but could pay great dividends for a single adult ministry.

Evangelism Conferences

Our single adult ministry sponsors two evangelism conferences—one in the spring and another in the fall. The program consists of one night of inspiration and witness training and one night of actually going out and witnessing. Preparations include enlisting a qualified inspirational speaker, a person to teach the basics of witnessing with a practice time, a committee to prepare a list of non-Christian single adults, a committee to publicize and enlist attendance at the evangelism conference, and a committee for fellowship and refreshments at break time. The suggested time schedule is 7 PM to 9 PM with two forty-five minute sessions with a thirty-minute break in the middle.

Single Adult Revival

The single adult revival can be local church, association, or citywide in scope. Preparations would be the same as for any church revival except that the target group would be single adults. Committees would be made up of single adults. The revival meeting could be held at the church. A central place would probably be more appropriate if more than one church was involved.

If a revival is done, it is urgent that a gifted speaker be used. Your success in revival will depend on adequate preparations which must include a list of single adult prospects. This means you may have to create a single adult prospect file. A singles search in your church will help. You do this by inserting a card in the Sunday bulletin for several weeks calling for the names (and appropriate information) of single adults. Invite all prospects to the revival. Be sure to have a fellowship time after each revival service. The suggested days for the revival are Sunday through Wednesday night. Most pastors will allow the single adults to be in charge of the Sunday night service in order to begin their revival.

Divorce Recovery Seminar

Twice a year we have a Divorce Recovery Seminar—Starting Over Again. We have one in March or April and one in October. The seminars have always paid for themselves. We have used two formats. For one seminar we use three Friday evenings in a row. On the first Friday evening a psychologist presents a seminar on "Building New Relationships," covering the subjects of dealing with depression, self-image, loneliness, and dating. This is followed by small discussion groups providing an opportunity to react to the presentation.

The second Friday evening a Christian psychologist presents a seminar on "How to Appropriate the Promises" covering the subject regarding both the spiritual and psychological aspects of singleness. This seminar is also followed by small-group sessions. Participants are encouraged to "talk it over" with a group of singles at a local restaurant afterward.

On the third Friday evening, our pastor presents what the Bible has to say about divorce and recovery. The third Friday evening is a banquet-type meeting. The schedule for the first and second Fridays is: 7 PM, registration and get acquainted; 7:30 PM, first session; 8:45 PM, break; 9:00 PM, small–group discussion; 9:45 PM, adjourn. Cost of the seminar was ten dollars whether one session or all. Banquet food was prepared by the church kitchen but could be catered.

The other seminar is done on a Friday evening and Saturday morning. Usually a Christian psychologist or qualified person is enlisted to do the whole series of seminars. The Friday night session is two hours. There is a continental breakfast on Saturday morning with two sessions, followed by a light noon meal before adjournment. Sometimes this person is used for a singles rally during the Sunday School hour. These two methods can be used to vary the format.

Any person who attends one of the divorce recovery seminars becomes an alumni. At the next one he pays no registration fee—just the cost of the meals, if any. This is important because this keeps the singles attending so they can become acquainted with the single prospects to enlist them in your church. We have found that we enlist about 35 percent of the prospects who attend the seminars.

It is important that you use every means possible for advertising, especially the local newspaper. Inadequate publicity will not provide enough prospects. Ask your church members to sponsor and enlist those who need help in this area.

28

Worship

GENE BOLIN

In my study is a box full of "junk mail," each piece promoting some new means of outreach or method of evangelism. It is truly amazing how something as simple as telling another person the wonderful good news of God's love as revealed through Jesus Christ has generated so many gimmicks, new techniques, and effortless methods. I suspect that if one wanted to be a full-time student of evangelism methodology, he could study until the second coming and never speak a word of the good news, having been so busy studying how to speak of the good news.

Evangelism is the proclamation of the good news of Jesus Christ for the purpose of bringing persons to accept and live by the redemptive love of God as revealed in Jesus Christ. Hence, if we are to evangelize, we must introduce persons to God and lead them into a personal relationship with Jesus. And we must lead those who have established a living, vital relationship with Christ into active involvement in the life of the Christian community—the church—where mutual encouragement and fellowship strengthens and prepares them for service both within and outside that community. Finally, we must enlist the collaborative efforts of new Christians to help bring every aspect of human life—private and social—under the rule of God.

One does not have to be a student of evangelism methodology

to be a good evangelist. One can invite unchurched friends to attend and participate in the worship service at a local church whereby they can experience the good news and be given the opportunity to respond in faith in Jesus Christ.

To be sure, worship is often viewed as speaking most to the Christian who comes to be strengthened, inspired, and encouraged. At the same time, however, worship, when it is biblically based, should enable the non-Christian to see, hear, and experience the reality of God, God's purpose for humankind, and the response God calls from each person who would fulfill that high destiny of fellowship with God.

When the church gathers to worship, it says to the world: "We acknowledge God as Creator, Redeemer, and Sustainer; we believe in one God, the Father, the Son, and the Holy Spirit; we accept Jesus Christ as Lord and Savior and are endeavoring to follow Christ, serve, and obey Him in the fellowship of this Church." And by maintaining the "unity of the Spirit in the bond of peace" (Eph. 4:3), the church embodies the fellowship (*koinonia*) which is theirs in Christ and which is the potential of all persons who trust him. Hence, worship can be a direct witness to the non-Christian who is invited to participate in worship; it is only an indirect witness to those who must observe a worshiping community from afar.

Worship, when properly planned and carried out, communicates the whole gospel message to which the non-Christian can respond in faith. Each element of the service leads to the next and adds to what it has contributed to the "message" of the hour so that when it comes to an end the sum total of the parts equals (or should equal) the communication and the experience of the good news of Jesus Christ.

Preparation for worship is a time for meditating and reflecting on the experience about to take place—the encounter with the living God. It is a time for shutting out the distractions and concerns of the world and for centering oneself, focusing on God, for in worship we offer to God ourselves in response to God's coming to us.

The *call to worship,* be it spoken or sung, is the means of announcing to those present that the worship of the living God is beginning. From this point on in the service, one's attention is focused on God and the response one can, should, and perhaps will make to God.

The *invocation* is the prayer voiced on behalf of the congregation asking God's blessing upon the service. It acknowledges the fact that the people are gathered to encounter the living God, to hear a word from the Lord, and to respond in loving obedience to God's will in the hours, days, and week ahead.

When we encounter God, we encounter God's holiness in contrast to our sinfulness. Hence, it is imperative that we acknowledge or *confess* our sinfulness and gratefully receive God's gracious *forgiveness.* This act in worship puts the Divine-human encounter into proper perspective. That which is wrong with us (sin) can only be made right (forgiven) by God—more particularly, by what God has provided for us through Jesus.

Praise naturally follows from the hearts and lips of those who have received from God what they could never provide for themselves—forgiveness and liberation from the awfulness of sin and its consequences. So with one voice we sing praises to God.

Proclamation of the Word will usually involve a sermon by the pastor. It may involve a drama, musical drama, or multimedia presentation. Always, however, it is based upon the biblical revelation and entails the application of biblical truths to the day-to-day experiences of the worshipers. It must always be a "word from the Lord" for today!

An opportunity to respond to the loving, unfolding will of God comes during the *invitation to Christian discipleship and time of commitment.* Proclamation will always speak to both the Christian and non-Christian; hence, the opportunity to respond will involve both.

An encounter with God is not only for the benefit of the worshiper but for the world for which God in Christ died. Having worshiped together, we naturally turn to each other to *share concerns and blessings.* It is during this part of the service that individuals voice their own prayer requests and share what God has been doing in their own lives. And it is a time when we intercede on behalf of those whose needs have been made known.

During the *offertory,* we give of our substance so that the work of the kingdom of God can be carried on through the church and around the world. The act of giving is a concrete way every worshiper can express his or her devotion to God and his or her commitment to the kingdom—"for where your treasure is, there will your heart be also" (Matt. 6:21).

Opportunities for service and growth in the coming week are announced, inviting each worshiper to give expression to his or her commitments through service to God through the church in the week ahead. All of us need spiritual refreshment in the middle of the week, and these opportunities are likewise announced.

The service is closed with a *benediction,* a prayer voiced on behalf of the congregation which asks God to bless what has just taken place and to enable persons to carry out the commitments made during the service through the power and strength of the Holy Spirit.

When worship is experienced in this way, it is a direct witness to the non-Christian. The experience of the service can be the occasion for conversation between Christian and non-Christian which can be used to heighten the personal application of the experience for both. The shared experience of worship becomes the focus of an extended and personalized witness.

It is relatively easy to invite non-Christian friends to worship with you when your church family gathers to worship each week. It is especially easy when the weekly experience speaks to the concerns you experience, when it addresses the issues you face as a single adult. It is normal and natural for friends to share their hopes and dreams, fears and frustrations. Worship can and should address the experiences that are common to all human beings. When it does, worship becomes an exciting experience, one that "speaks to me"—and one that must be shared with others like me.

Someone has likened witnessing to "one beggar telling another beggar where to find bread." When worship feeds us on the Bread of life, you can be confident that there are many others in your world who are eager to taste of the same loaf!

The worship service can be enough of an experience to draw persons to Christ in faith. Worship plus person-centered conversation focusing on the worship experience is even better. Hence, Christian single adults who bring friends with them to worship can extend the witness of the worship experience by talking about that experience with their friends. What did you think about

. . . ? How did you feel when . . . ? In which parts of the service did you experience God's presence? What do you think was the point of the sermon? What response do you think the pastor was asking you to make? How urgent do you believe the pastor felt that response was? What difference would that response make in your life? All such questions are normal outgrowths of any worship experience; all can provide a wonderfully natural opening to share a personalized witness.

You need not be a student of evangelism methodology to be an effective witness. You can use the several worship opportunities your church provides each week to invite non-Christian friends. And you can follow up those experiences by discussing them to their ultimate conclusion: personal response to the living God. After all, that is what worship is all about: Encounter God, respond to God.

29
Revival Meetings

JOEY HANCOCK

The revival meeting in the local church is a time-proven tool for reaching unsaved and unchurched people and for rekindling the hearts of Christians. These are times of excitement and enrichment in the life of any church. Throughout the years, Southern Baptists have greatly reaped the blessings of revival meetings. There is no better time or place to involve Christian singles in the life of the local church than during a revival meeting. By placing Christian singles into the fabric of our revival preparation, we will be enriching both the church and the lives of these single believers.

As you look across the congregation of your church, you will see many singles who can be great resources in planning, preparing, and promoting a revival meeting. In any form of revival preparation, involvement of people is the key. As more and more people become involved, every aspect of the meeting will become better. The most wonderful blessings of the meeting for those involved will come when the actual meeting begins, while they are busy working for the Lord. Perhaps the best way of involvement is through the use of committees. There are committees that form a solid platform of preparation for the meeting. Have you ever thought about placing some key singles on one or more of these committees?

Beaming with enthusiasm and creativity, singles can make excellent committee members. The basic committees needed for most church revivals would be prayer, publicity, telephone, attendance, music, visitation, ushers, children, counseling, and follow-up. As needed, you could either change or add committees.

As a committee member, each key single should also be working out ways to involve other singles in the committee's work. Each committee will have two basic functions. First, they must supply the creative touch to identify their goals. Each committee should have a specific goal. Secondly, this committee must design a strategy to reach this goal. So creativity and carrying out are two important factors of this committee involvement. The singles in your church know specific talents that each possesses and often can recommend a particular person for a particular task. In your selection of these key singles, try to select a single who is involved and knows a number of other singles. By this method, they can reach those who are less involved. As this revival meeting becomes their meeting, instead of another meeting that the church is having, these singles will find themselves more eager to attend and support the meeting.

During a revival meeting is a good time to enrich the many ministries of our church. One is the music ministry. Some singles are in the gap between the youth choir and the adult choir. During the week of revival, most churches have a revival choir. By inviting singles into this choir, you can encourage them to come on into the choir for their age after the meeting. Also, the revival meeting is a great time to have singles sing in special duets, ensembles, or solos. This is a prime time to involve these dynamic people further in the ministry of the church.

Up until now we have discussed involving the already churched single in the revival meeting. Another single must now come into our focus. This is the unsaved and/or unchurched single. As

Christians, we have the answer that each of these singles is searching for: Jesus Christ. Therefore, the sum total of our planning and preparing is to reach these folks with the gospel. In our society, as fast paced and busy as it is, we must reach out with clear-cut objectives and strategies in mind to reach people for Christ. During times of revival meetings, many people are reached for the Lord. Your church revival meeting will be a valuable tool to reach this group of singles, if you so prepare.

As singles are involved in the planning of strategies for the meeting, you will see ways in which your church can reach the non-Christian single. After instilling a vision to reach out in our singles, we then must cultivate their desires and provide a structure in which they can carry out their plans. You might want to have a special night of the revival called Singles' Night. This night should be discussed in the planning meeting of the attendance committee and then promoted. The purpose of this night would be to have a special emphasis to reach a special group of people.

First, the target group would be established. Who are we going to target our work toward? In the development of this strategy, this group must clearly be defined. After this group is targeted, then the ways to reach them are discussed. The revival service that evening should be geared to this group. Ask the evangelist to preach a message in this area. Share your goals with the musician for the week and have him structure the music to appeal to this group. Perhaps a single soloist could sing or a single ensemble could share. Then ask the pastor about a single giving a testimony that evening. You might even consider bringing in a single personality for a testimony that evening.

After the service, plan a single fellowship and pull out all the stops to make it a great evening. The guest evangelist might drop by and answer questions about subjects that the singles are concerned about. The news of this special night should be placed in places where it will reach the target group. Extra work in carrying out the invitations will result in more people coming to the Lord.

Visitation is essential in reaching this target group of unsaved and/or unchurched singles for the Lord. The Sunday School is the best place to base your work. Have the Singles Department plan a Sunday School visitation effort. This effort could be a special night for visitation, a number of visitation dates set for

144

more convenient visiting, or a handout of cards with names and addresses of prospects for each to visit. Beginning a home Bible study for singles prior to the revival would help provide a place in which to cultivate the prospect. By getting to know the group, the prospect would find it easier to make your church his home.

Prayer certainly is a key to any movement of God. We can never overemphasize the need to pray. As you develop a special prayer strategy for singles, remember your target group and have them pray specifically for this group. Prayer cells meeting weekly prior to the revival is a powerful way to challenge singles to pray. By developing a prayer partner concept, you will add a depth of love and concern for the unsaved and unchurched. As they pray, not only will God honor their prayers for the lost, but also this group will grow spiritually. After all, isn't this what revival is all about?

Many think that participation in a revival meeting is to come and receive a blessing and go home. Through the methods and concepts that we have discussed in this chapter, you have seen that to participate in a revival meeting means to get involved. Our singles are ready to get involved, if you and I will help them. The Lord said to pray for the laborers because the harvest is plentiful. Our singles are the laborers, so let's enlist them and equip them to go into the harvest for the Lord.

30

Support Groups

DONNA H. POYNOR

At first glance, it might seem that the support group is a twentieth-century phenomenon that has come about through the proliferation of the practice of psychotherapy. The type of group we shall consider in this chapter, however, has its origin not in modern psychotherapy but rather in the life and ministry of Jesus Christ. It was He who called the twelve to share life with Him, to learn, and grow together. And it was He who commanded His followers to love one another, to bear one another's burdens, and

145

to carry the good news of His saving love to the uttermost parts of the earth. The support group is a vehicle through which these commandments may be obeyed.

Even with its origin in the first century (or perhaps even earlier), there is no doubt that the support group has become increasingly popular among Christians in recent years. Literally thousands of participants in these small groups are recipients of revival and renewal that have occurred as they have come to a new and deeper understanding of their relationship with God, themselves, and others by sharing life with fellow believers in a support group setting.

What accounts for this explosion of small groups? Findley Edge, in the introduction to *Growth Through Groups* by William Clemmons and Harvey Hester, wrote, "The emergence of the small group on the current scene was a spontaneous phenomenon in which one, whose life was enriched by this experience, shared with another what was happening in his life. In this manner, the movement has spread like wildfire across our nation. Why has the small group experience merged and grown so rapidly at this particular time? Some of us believe that the Holy Spirit of God has been in it giving leadership, direction, and power."[1]

As both a participant in and an observer of support groups over the past fifteen years, I could not agree more! It is a profound and beautiful experience for believers to discover in a dynamic way the presence of God and the power of the Holy Spirit in their lives through the sharing of those lives at a significant level with others in a small group. And what a joyous happening it is when a nonbeliever comes to know Christ as Savior through the small-group experience! The validity of the support group as a tool for renewal and revival among God's people is being affirmed daily and we need to thank Him for it.

The support group has special significance in single adult ministry. Because of their great mobility, single adults perhaps more than any other group often do not live in proximity to their natural support groups, their families. In the case of the single again, families have been disrupted. In addition, we are faced with the increasing impersonalization of our society and, sadly, of our churches as well. When Christianity becomes impersonal, more conceptual than experiential, a void exists in the believer's life. The support group can be the instrument God uses to help us fill that void with the reality of His presence in us and others.

An appropriate goal for a support group is the personal growth of each individual emotionally, relationally, intellectually, and spiritually. In his book *Growth Groups* Howard Clinebell suggests that a group aim at a balanced emphasis on the three interdependent dimensions of human development—inreach, outreach, and upreach. Clinebell says, "Inreach refers to growth in awareness—coming alive to oneself. The walls between us are extensions of the walls within us. Inreach means relating responsibly and responsively to oneself—taking one's own feelings and needs seriously. Outreach means relating responsibly and responsively to others. Upreach refers to growth of a stronger, more trustful connection with the vertical dimension—with the Source of all life and growth."[2]

As you think about organizing support groups in your church, it is important to realize that you may already have some that are functioning, but under different names. We often limit ourselves to thinking about the relational group when we consider support groups. Two other types are identified by Em Griffin in *Getting Together.* Task groups are those formed to accomplish a job which can't be done by one person alone.[3] An example might be a single adult council. It is not at all unusual for a group called into existence to perform a task to become, through time spent together working toward a common goal, a support group. The other type Griffin defines is the influence group. It is composed of people who admit the need for change in their lives. They voluntarily gather and request that others exhort them and have an impact on their behavior and attitudes. Examples of this type of group are Alcoholics Anonymous and Weight Watchers. In the Christian community, a witnessing seminar is the type of influence group that often evolves into a support group.[4]

And don't forget the Sunday night "let's-get-something-to-eat-after-church" group. If participants in this activity are essentially the same week after week, there is real potential for this to become a support group known by no name at all! So, before you set out to involve people in support groups, recognize that some may already be involved in task or influence groups that are, indeed, filling this need in their lives.

147

The relational group is the one we most often refer to as a support group. It has as its expressed purpose the growth of the individual through interpersonal interaction with group members. For the group to achieve optimal effectiveness, the interaction must be carried on with each person being as honest about his or her feelings as it is possible to be at any given time. It is this type of group that will likely prove most useful for the single adult who is trying to come to terms with singleness, and for the single again person who is dealing with loss, anger, rejection, and the many related emotions that follow the loss of a spouse through death or divorce. This is also the type of group that can serve very effectively as an outreach tool to the non-Christian single adult. For many of them, the turning point may be when they are able to share their thoughts and feelings without fear of condemnation, and when they are able to see their Christian friends being real, having left their religious masks at home, but still showing evidence of Christ living in them.

Support groups of the relational variety may be organized according to categories of singleness (never married, divorced, widowed, separated, single parent), interests, or common needs and concerns. While the goals of each of these will be very similar, the initial approach and choice of materials to be used (if any) will probably vary. For example, a group formed of people who find themselves in the role of single parent will most likely spend more time in the beginning sharing parenting experiences and trying to establish that "I'm not the only one with this particular problem," whereas a group formed from a common interest in studying the Bible with other Christians and relating around that base will probably choose to begin with a study of Scripture and move from there into the sharing of personal experience.

In terms of evangelistic outreach, groups formed to help meet needs of those going through a divorce or those who have lost a spouse to death are extremely effective. Hurting people come to these groups, many out of desperation, looking for any kind of help they can find. When they encounter leaders who genuinely care and people who are experiencing the same upheaval that they are but have the resource of Christ living in them to help them through it, they have in many instances found what has been missing in their struggle. Because of the help they have received in dealing with their emotional trauma, many have come into the kingdom of God.

The following are some things to consider as you organize support groups:

1. Have a schedule. Sessions should be frequent enough so that time is not wasted at each session "catching up" and getting "reconnected." Weekly sessions of one and a half to two hours seem to work well. Agree to honor the time limit. An occasional marathon session may occur, but it should be the exception.

2. Set a closing date. People are reluctant to make open-ended commitments. Agree to meet for a specified length of time (eight to twelve weeks is reasonable) and then to determine as a group if the meetings should continue.

3. Limit the size of the group. Effective communication and sharing at deep levels will probably not occur with more than eight people present.

4. Don't add people after the second session. If people are added in each session, the initial "getting to know you" stage will be extended to a point where significant sharing may never take place.

5. Find a meeting place. It should be private enough so that interruptions are minimal and comfortable enough to encourage growth work. Meeting in homes of members will work well so long as no one feels a burden to be host or hostess.

6. Set group goals and establish other guidelines together. The group will need to agree upon certain principles and make commitments to each other concerning such things as attendance, confidentiality, openness, honesty, sensitivity, and personal accountability, to name a few.

How are such groups started? They usually begin when one or more persons expresses a need for others with whom to share life at more than a superficial level. They begin out of a common concern, need, or interest. They may begin from a shared sense of mission. In the framework of the church, you may simply want to announce that a small group is being formed for the purpose of helping individuals grow emotionally, relationally, intellectually, and spiritually. Church members should be encouraged to invite non-Christian friends as they deem it appropriate. For a group to succeed, the people must have some common identity, have a common goal, want to be together, be able to laugh and cry together, be willing to leave their "masks" at home, and affirm each other as they grow together and seek the leadership of the Holy Spirit.

In *The Dynamics of Small Groups Within the Church,* Bill Vaughn writes, "The small group within the church is a God-instrument that helps each member toward God's goal of Christlikeness in inner spirit and in one's total outer behavior. The small group within the church is a God-instrument that encourages each member to grow in Christian characteristics and toward his fullest potential as a useful person in the world community. The small group within the church is a God-instrument that challenges each member to reach one hand up to God and the other hand in loving outreach to all one's fellowmen. The small group is ministry!"[5]

1. William Clemmons and Harvey Hester, *Growth Through Groups* (Nashville: Broadman Press, 1974), p. 13.

2. Howard Clinebell, *Growth Groups* (Nashville: Abingdon, 1972), p. 5.

3. Em Griffin, *Getting Together* (Downers Grove, Illinois: Inter-Varsity Press, 1982), pp. 27-32.

4. Ibid., p. 39.

5. Bill Vaughn, *The Dynamics of Small Groups within the Church* (Kansas City, Missouri: Beacon Hill Press of Kansas City, 1980), pp. 11-12.

31

Visitation

DEBORAH ANNE MURRELL

The church of the twentieth century finds itself confronting new problems and new methods of reaching persons with the Word of God. Many of these problems are due to the fast rate of change. There is change in education, in the manner of work, in advertisement, in the nuclear family, and in the structure of the local church. Since there are more single adults in America than at any other time in history, this also poses a problem to the local church. How can the church minister to persons who do not fit the general pattern of church structure? These are only a few of the problems which the church faces today. The church has only one choice. Either it can reach out to these areas of needs and minister, or it can adopt the technological philosophy, "Ignore the needs and they will go away."

During the days of the early church there were many peoples in the world; but the church was unique, a divinely constituted "new people," the possession of God. It was sent to proclaim God's goodness and love, to be a witness to God's condescension in history, and to have a part in claiming for its God men and women from every race, tongue, and nation. The New Testament refers to the church as a people, as God's people. Today the people of God need to catch a vision as to the scope of the ministry of the early church, and to implement that vision into a new vision for the world today. Old ideas in a technological world, led by the Holy Spirit, create a new sense of commitment and evangelism.

How are the people of God today going to carry forth the Great Commission? Paul stated it best in Romans 10:14-15: "How then shall they call upon Him in whom they have not believed? And how shall they believe in Him whom they have not heard? And how shall they hear without a preacher? And how shall they preach unless they are sent? Just as it is written, 'HOW BEAUTI-FUL ARE THE FEET OF THOSE WHO BRING GLAD TID-INGS OF GOOD THINGS!' " As we go into our city (Jerusalem), reach forth to an urban society (Judea), daily meet the needs of those we encounter (Samaria), we *will* be His witnesses, "even to the remotest parts of the earth" (Acts 1:8).

But how can we do this? An effective ministry of both outreach and inreach will develop a warm and loving fellowship within the church, and this is labeled "around reach." For revival to occur through visitation, a renewal of one's faith and an awareness of an in-depth meaning to life needs to take place. Various programs of outreach have been developed, but none of them will be effectively employed within the church without a personal renewal in one's relationship with the living God.

Through single adult ministry within the local church, the following plan can become an effective tool for meeting needs, renewal, and revival.

Outreach Visitation

Know Your Visitors

An effective outreach/visitation leader will meet as many visitors on Sunday as possible. Two co-outreach leaders for overall singles ministry are effective. Not only do they arrive twenty minutes early on Sunday, but they also work with the church outreach director, individual classes, and the single adult minister or educational minister.

Organization for Visitation

The church outreach director is responsible for organizing the visitation program. By obtaining the registration slips from Sunday School and compiling the names of visitors who signed the church guest books, the outreach director completes the prospect/visitor cards for distribution on Tuesday night. Often church members will submit the names of persons who are single and are personal friends or family members. After the names are recorded, they are sorted according to geographical location. By meeting at 6:00 PM, there is sufficient time to go over the assignments and to pray together as a group.

Making a Personal Visit

Always have a New Testament (Psalms and Proverbs) with you. A personal working knowledge of the Scriptures and a sensitivity to the Holy Spirit's leading is preeminent for effective visitation. Because God is at work in you, He will effectively use you as His tool. This is the catalyst for revival. Revival comes in the overflow of one's life! As we progressively grow in our Christian life, we will want to plant seeds and to invest ourselves in the lives of others.

The first visit is an "appreciation" visit. It is a time to be sensitive to the needs of the one who is being visited. What could be more exciting than having a prospect say, "Oh, I was hoping that someone from the church would come to see me!" This becomes an "open door" for effectively being sensitive to their needs.

Have a listening ear. (Sit near the prospect, not on the opposite side of the room). What needs are being expressed? Mental? Social? Physical? Spiritual? Financial? Is this person new to the community? To which category(ies) of singleness does he or she relate? What is the person's spiritual background?

For the single adult prospect who does not know Christ as personal Savior, be ready to share the plan of salvation. There are many effective tools that can be used: Four Spiritual Laws, Roman Road, Continual Witness Training, Evangelism Explosion, or EvangeLife. Training sessions in any of these methodologies prior to visitation is essential to an awareness of the need for a personal relationship with Jesus Christ before you complete the visit.

In visiting the single adult who is already a Christian, lead the person to share his journey with you. Listen for continual growth or for pauses in the growth. For many, this visit is one of "new beginnings!" It is here that excitement grows. As you share, you may discover similarities. Be aware of the fact that a friendship could form. Who knows! This person may be another visitation partner. Give encouragement when needed. This is a tool of the Holy Spirit for growth. Have prayer with the person before you leave. Also, leave your name and phone number, as well as the phone number of your church. A few days after making a visit, give the person a phone call. Be genuine. Be sincere. Discuss the possibility of another visit and make the appointment.

Follow Through

After visiting, meet the other visitation teams at church for a time of sharing, prayer, and fellowship. Everyone will have something to share; some will be excited over the response to the gospel, while others may need encouragement or insight. Others may simply share a burden or a need. Visitation support systems are important.

Share the visits you make with Sunday School teachers and/or the pastor. Complete the prospect/visitor card and return it to the outreach director.

If visitation is thought of in terms of an investment, then revival becomes the dividend. The greater the emphasis on visitation and doing it, the greater the growth rate in the local church.

Inreach Visitation

Inreach visitation promotes growth within small groups. Each group has a leader with no more than six or seven persons per group. These groups can consist of persons within the same categories of singleness, or they can be from different categories. The prime purpose of these groups is personal growth and healing. As growth and healing occur, a desire will develop to reach out to new persons and to visit with them.

Other Resources

Conduct a "person survey" with single adults who are currently attending Sunday School. Enlist their assistance for names of friends, neighbors, and relatives who would be prospects.

Consult with local utility companies for new persons moving into the area. Many provide this information to churches as a community service.

Apartment managers may release the names of persons who have recently moved into their complexes.

The local board of education may release the names of single teachers new to their school system.

A Concluding Thought

Jesus' ministry on earth was relational—one on one as well as with small groups. He *trained* the disciples. They came to know Him and follow Him; they spoke boldly about the New Life which Christ had given to them! "And with great power the apostles were giving witness to the resurrection of the Lord Jesus, and abundant grace was upon them all" (Acts 4:33). Person to person, door to door, on the job, off the job, we are to work in His fields until He comes again. The fields are ready for harvesting. Persons are waiting for us to reach out to them in their need.

Single adults are mobile. Their life-style is independent and flexible. They are seeking God's will. They are discovering that His will is to know Him and to share that relationship with others. Once single adults come to know Christ, they become willing to share the abundant life. They will make time in their weekly schedule for visitation and phone calls. Nothing will bring joy quicker to a pastor than to see persons sharing Christ with others. Happy is the church that reaches out and brings persons within!

32

Conferences and Retreats

TIM CLEARY

Each single adult held a helium-filled balloon with a personal message of confession and commitment attached. One by one the balloons were released into the heavens, symbolically carrying with them the things that held back revival in individuals' lives. Some professed Christ. Others shared the release of resentment and previously unyielded life circumstances. Through the medium of a creative worship and commitment service, a carefully planned, prayed for, and orchestrated single adult conference was concluding with an outward demonstration of God's Spirit at work.

We as leaders can set the stage for single adults, one of the largest unchurched population groups (41 percent unchurched compared to 29 percent of marrieds unchurched),[1] to find initial and renewed faith in Jesus Christ through the ministry of conferences and retreats. To prepare for this, we must have a vision, enter into faith partnerships with singles and their leaders, develop and work a plan, generate the right spirit, anticipate spiritual fruit, follow up responsibly, and celebrate the results.

Vision. "Where there is no vision, the people perish" (Prov. 29:18, KJV). Have you ever been the victim of faulty thinking that says, "Let's throw together a conference to keep the singles from complaining that the church never does anything for them?" A trend in single adult work has many churches planning a conference or retreat as a substitute for ongoing quality programming. A leader must pray for and develop God's vision for a total ministry with single adults, then catch a vision of where conferences and retreats fit into this scheme. As this is done, each

155

conference event will develop its own unique vision of God's working as it relates to an ongoing ministry.

The word *vision* implies creativity within the context of a total picture. Develop a total picture for your event by seeking direction from and asking God these questions: What are the key areas of need for the singles we will relate to? Which needs should we target and how should we do so? What resource persons has God gifted in such a way that they could speak to these needs? What spiritual outcome do we desire and how can we relate that to our ongoing ministry? What theme would capsulize our desired outcome? What frameworks could be designed for our outcome to be achieved? Who within our group can be counted on to help us detail, enlarge, and carry out this vision?

I believe that once the visions of *why, what, which,* and *whom* are conceptualized, then the *how, when,* and *what next* can be effectively addressed. This beginning creative visualizing becomes a reference point for further planning.

Faith Partnerships. "Every purpose is established by counsel" (Prov. 20:18, KJV). The greatest spiritual revivals in church history have had their roots planted in the soil of shared vision. Recall with me the prayer meeting outlined in Acts 1:12-14 that resulted in the Pentecost of Acts 2. Here, a small committed core of believers gathered to share a common vision in one accord, in prayer, and supplication, seeking God's anointing. Gather a core group of persons to seek counsel from and develop detailed plans with. This may be an established planning group such as a single adult council, or it may be an ad hoc committee of singles and their leaders.

Practical results of including others in preparation for your event are: 1) Greater participation as those involved in planning reach out and invite others. 2) Better division of logistics as more persons share tasks. 3) More enthusiasm for accomplishing assigned tasks as you encourage one another. 4) Increased spiritual preparation as planners pray individually and together for the event and participants.

While one person alone can be an effective leader and witness, there is something special to be accomplished through Christ's presence by a council. Let's allow God to use us in twos, threes, or more as we make plans for singles to come to our conference seeking Him.

Develop and Work a Plan. "For God so loved the world, that He gave His only begotten Son, that whoever believes in Him should not perish, but have eternal life" (John 3:16). God had a vision for our redemption, developing a master plan to see it through. We can also bring God's redemptive plan to bear in the lives of singles as we utilize this example in our planning.

As you plan become aware of the characteristics and needs of singles outlined in *How to Start a Single Adult Ministry.*[2] This will enhance your ability to relate the content most effectively to persons attending. Related to this are two crucial redemptive issues to be addressed which play an important role in bringing the spirit of revival to your event.

First, single adults need to feel loved. They will come seeking a caring fellowship, looking for insight into how to love others and better accept themselves, or perhaps looking for that "special someone." Utilize this as an opportunity to share throughout your program the message of God's *agape* love in Christ from which all other love relationships flow. Accomplish this by: 1) Providing ample time and opportunity for getting acquainted. 2) Scheduling seminars related to love, intimacy, self-esteem, relationship building, sexuality, interpersonal communication skills, and marriage preparation. 3) Allowing worship experiences to be expressions of God's love through music, testimonies, prayer, creative participation, preaching topics, and commitment opportunities. 4) Develop and use "listening teams" of caring persons who will be sensitive, ministering to those who are lonely and isolated from others.

Secondly, many who come will feel as though they have perished or are about to. These include among others recently separated or divorced persons, the newly widowed, never marrieds discontented with their status, and single parents under financial or emotional duress. Programming that can bring positive renewal to this group, helping them realize that it is not God's plan for them to perish, includes: 1) Fellowship and support groups in which to share common needs. 2) Counseling opportunities with faculty, other leaders, and in response to decision services. 3) Topical seminars on grief, divorce adjustment, parenting skills,

157

dealing with emotions, coping with crisis (such as mid-life), and forgiveness. 4) Emphasis in worship, especially speakers' topics, focusing on one's need to be responsible for oneself in responding to God's *love, grace, forgiveness,* and *redemptive power.*

Generate the Right Spirit. "I have come that they might have life and have it abundantly" (John 10:10). Part of evangelizing the single adult population today is challenging them to see the "good news" of the gospel. Singles, especially the growing group of highly articulate, professionally skilled persons, do not want to attend pity parties planned for social lepers by well-meaning persons wanting to help them live with their affliction until they marry into wholeness. Therefore, through our publicity materials, format, and faculty, we must generate the right spirit by presenting the Christian life-style as positive, adventuresome, exciting, and fulfilling for singles. Key things to remember here are: 1) Design publicity and other materials that are colorful and attractive. 2) Budget enough money to effectively communicate with the target group you seek to reach. 3) Utilize target and direct mailers to reach singles in the community as well as your church. 4) Organize phone volunteers who will share personal invitations to attend. 5) Enlist conference leaders who understand, relate, and can challenge single adults intellectually and spiritually. 6) Speak positively to and solicit the support of the entire church and its staff in praying for and promoting the event.

Anticipate Spiritual Fruit. "So shall my Word . . . not return to Me empty,/Without accomplishing what I desire" (Isa. 55:11). If we believe this we will provide times for both public and private expression of commitment as part of our event. We shouldn't number it for numbers' sake, compare it, or artificially produce it; but we should anticipate and prepare for it by keeping in mind: 1) Provide for a public invitation and adequate counseling. 2) Provide an appropriate plan and space for receiving persons. 3) Record important information on decisions for further follow up. 4) Alert helping professionals to be available for crisis counsel. 5) Communicate in advance with speakers as to the number of times and method of public invitations. 6) Kindle flames of expectation in faculty and participants through prayer experiences.

Follow Up Responsibly and Celebrate the Results. "Rejoicing in hope, persevering in tribulation, devoted to prayer" (Rom. 12:12).

1) Openly rejoice with those whose lives have been transformed. Encourage their church and Christian friends to minister to them. 2) Persevere with those whose pain is so great that they could not experience personal victory at this time by practicing the ministry of encouragement to them. 3) Prayerfully evaluate with your partners in faith planning each aspect of the conference experience. Ideas for follow-through on the preceding include: 1) Sending an affirming letter to those making decisions. 2) Placing their names on prospect and ministry lists. 3) Planning specific outreach times to contact prospects who attended the event. 4) Arranging for testimonies in church services by participants and planners.

Let us accept the challenge as leaders to pray and plan for "an extraordinary movement of the Holy Spirit, producing extraordinary results."[3] *A Conference Leader's Prayer:* Go ye into the conference or retreat and share good news with every single one you meet. Plans baptized with the Spirit's power, claiming victories for each hour. Sharing love, hope and grace, helping singles see His face.

1. Gallup Organization, *Religion in America.* Princeton: 1981.

2. Ann Alexander Smith, *How to Start a Single Adult Ministry.* Nashville: Baptist Sunday School Board Church Literature Order 9804-8, 1980.

3. Richard Owen Roberts, *Revival.* Wheaton, IL: Tyndale House Inc., 1982, pp. 16-17.

Study Helps

1. John L. Casteel, *Renewal in Retreats.* New York: Association Press, 1959.
2. Lynn and Virgil Nelson, *Retreat Handbook, A-Way to Meaning.* Valley Forge: Judson Press, 1976.
3. Frank Hart Smith, *A Guide to Planning and Conducting a Retreat.* Nashville: Convention Press, 1977.

33

Discipleship Training

BILLY JUSTISS

"For the equipping of the saints for the work of service, to the building up of the body of Christ" (Eph. 4:12).

One of the common criticisms of churches today is the overlooking of discipleship training for the people who are already believers. This is a justifiable complaint, and it isn't new in the history of our churches.

On a summer Sunday night in 1953, as a senior high student, I accepted Jesus Christ as my Savior. This, of course, has been an unforgettable time in my life. No one said to me, "OK, Billy, as a Christian, you need to begin on a spiritual journey of growing through life."

We cannot become disciplers until we have been trained through our own down-to-earth handling of difficulties and frustrations of life. This growth is obtainable through seminars, retreats, Christian training hour, single families Bible study groups, and the Sunday morning Bible study. We *must* encourage our brothers and sisters in Christ to grow through those situations, not grope in them.

I personally define the discipleship ministry of our singles as the "Shepherd Ministry" and the support group as the "Jethro Program."

With these ministries, our singles are encouraged to become involved. Through a singles survey, we discover their spiritual gifts. Through our Jethro Program, singles can support the ministries by using their natural talents or motivational gifts.

When Christian singles have become involved in discipleship training through ministries, they will share Jesus Christ in their daily life-style because their life-style will be one of an evangelist.

To introduce our ministry of discipleship for the result of revival, we need to define discipleship. My personal interpretation would be to ask two questions: Are you involved in any form of evangelism? Are you setting an example by your "walk and talk" (Col. 4:5-6)?

These are fulfilled by teaching a Bible study class, by participating in discussion groups, witnessing seminars or discipleship studies, and organized church visitation, and by letting the Holy Spirit lead you in your daily walk to share the good news.

What is a disciple?

1. A believer in Jesus Christ as Lord and Savior of one's life (John 3:16; Rom. 10:9-13).

2. A believer obedient to the command to go and, while going, to witness (Matt. 28:18-20).

3. A believer who abides in Christ (John 15).

4. A believer who desires to learn (Col. 2:6-7).

5. A believer who has a desire to fellowship with believers (Heb. 10:24-25; 1 John 1:3).

6. A believer who desires to minister to needs of individuals (Acts 2:44-45).

Discipleship is characterized by:

1. Application of the gifts of the Spirit in our life to glorify Jesus Christ (Rom. 12:6-8).

2. Demonstration of the fruit of the Spirit in our daily walk in the form of life-style evangelism (Gal. 5:22-23,25).

3. A desire to share Jesus Christ with the non-Christian (Mark 16:15).

Discipleship requires:

1. Responsibility (John 8:31; 2 Tim. 2:1-2).

2. Love (John 13:34-35).

3. Abiding in Christ (John 15:5).

Discipleship ingredients: dedicated service—deny self, take up cross daily, and follow Jesus Christ (Luke 9:23).

The biblical pattern is involvement in both evangelism and discipling while we are ministering to others. The church should offer the opportunity to be involved in carrying out the Great Commission through the strengthening of our faith, personal growth as an individual and family, and opportunities for Christian service.

You will notice that reaching (evangelism) and teaching (discipleship) are continuous as the ministering (service) is applied to the completeness of reaching and teaching.

• Reaching (Evangelism)—Acts 5:28. Evangelism brings new life into a ministry; it is the key to discipling. If a believer does not have the gift of witnessing, we are told to train him so he may share with boldness.

• Teaching (Discipleship)—Hebrews 6:1-2. Teachers must demonstrate Bible study methods and model the Christian life in their giving, sharing, ministering, fellowshipping, and witnessing.

• Ministering (Serving)—Galatians 5:13; 1 John 3:18-19. Close relationships are developed as we minister to non-Christians and believers. Ministering helps bridge the gap between the non-Christians and Christ as they see love from us. Ministering also strengthens the believers when we are involved through the love of ministering.

Discipleship training helps a person realize his potential through Christ. His self-esteem is raised as he sees that he is worth something to the Master. Many singles need this good self-esteem.

We have to get single Christians to realize that they can and should serve others while needing to take care of their own needs and to love others as they are growing in loving themselves. Jesus, on the cross, was concerned enough to tell the apostle John to take care of Mary.

We need to minister to the singles' needs related to divorce, self-esteem, dating, sexuality, relationships, God's will, single parenting, and stress, but the key is encouraging them to become involved in ministry.

Before we present ministries that promote revival through discipleship training, let's briefly define how revival comes: as renewal *reviving*, it comes when one person or group of persons catches a vision of what God wants and as that vision is passed on and on until revival takes place. It's contagious.

The Shepherd Ministry is a threefold ministry of: 1) reaching the non-Christian ("Rod") by reaching, sharing, praying; 2) discipling the Christian ("Staff") by training, helping, encouraging; and 3) ministering to fellow believers ("Comforter") by loving, caring, bearing.

Revival through discipleship training is: 1) A pastor preaching the gospel, encouraging the nonbeliever to accept Jesus Christ as Lord and the Christian to a life of commitment; 2) Bible teaching from teachers who believe the Sunday morning Bible study is the end result of a week of "I love you" ministry; 3) single leaders growing by becoming involved in witnessing, visiting, ministering, and praying; and 4) singles ministers encouraging singles to be involved in life-style evangelism by "walking the walk and talking the talk" daily in the marketplace of their world.

Part V

Challenge for Revival Among Single Adults

34

From a Single Adult

F. MAURINE FREEZE

We have listened with interest to stories of great revivals and spiritual awakenings of the past, and we are excited about the possibility of revival happening again. Everywhere Christians are talking about the need for revival and praying we will experience the dynamic reality of a personal spiritual renewal.

With the church's acceptance of singleness as a valid life-style comes an awareness of the vast potential single adults have for evangelistic purposes in Southern Baptist churches. We who work with singles recognize within our single adult membership an untapped resource to be used for the purpose of revival. We need to capitalize on this asset.

Revival originates with God. He longs to revive His children. He yearns to manifest His power and presence in our lives. "The eyes of the Lord move to and fro throughout the earth that He may strongly support those whose heart is completely His" (2 Chron. 16:9).

Revival begins with a renewed life. God begins with an individual, working progressively through that person to usher in revival on a larger scale. There will be no corporate revival in our churches until individual members are revived.

An awareness of need is the first condition for renewal to occur in the life of a believer. Realizing something is missing, the individual cries out for the fullness of God. A hunger and thirst for righteousness is displayed. "Blessed are those who hunger and thirst for righteousness, for they shall be satisfied" (Matt. 5:6).

Upon recognition of my need for renewal, I literally cried out to God. My days were consumed with prayer and Bible study as I sought the Lord. One day the break came. While attending a prayer meeting in the home of a friend, I began to sense the presence of God in a way as never before. As deep conviction swept over me, my heart became broken over personal sins.

An acknowledgment of sin always precedes renewal. Confession is agreeing with God concerning sin. It is saying what He says about the sin in our lives. "For all have sinned and fall short of the glory of God" (Rom. 3:23).

As we recognize conflicts and admit failures, we are to confess. One by one, individual sins are acknowledged to God, as we claim the promise, "If we confess our sins, He is faithful and righteous to forgive us our sins and to cleanse us from all unrighteousness" (1 John 1:9).

Our past is a living part of our present. Unless we deal scripturally with past failures, we will not be able to experience the renewed life God makes possible to all who meet His conditions.

Confession involves reconciliation with others. Some argue, "Isn't confession to God enough?" No, my friend. Until you are willing to be reconciled with those whom you have offended, you will never know the reality of renewal. "If therefore you are presenting your offering at the altar, and there remember that your brother has something against you, leave your offering there before the altar, and go your way; first be reconciled to your brother, and then come and present your offering" (Matt. 5:23-24).

The greatest barrier to seeking forgiveness is pride. It is not easy to admit failure. When we humble ourselves in obedience to God, we receive the grace necessary to seek forgiveness.

To forgive others is a choice we make. It is an act of the will. I am choosing to make forgiveness my life-style. One of my personal goals is found in Acts 24:16, "In view of this, I also do my best to maintain always a blameless conscience both before God and before men."

We receive forgiveness to the degree we are willing to forgive.

"For if you forgive men for their transgressions, your heavenly Father will also forgive you. But if you do not forgive men, then your Father will not forgive your transgressions" (Matt. 6:14-15).

Another condition of renewal is abandonment to God. The essence of abandonment is unconditional surrender. Surrender is giving God freedom to do as He chooses with your life. It is allowing His will to become your will.

Sometimes God uses circumstances to bring His children to a place of surrender. These circumstances can be very painful. He used the fragmenting circumstances of divorce to bring me to confess my sins, to mend broken relationships, and to make restitution where possible.

How does one surrender? The answer is found in Romans 12:1-2, "I urge you therefore, brethren, by the mercies of God, to present your bodies a living and holy sacrifice, acceptable to God, which is your spiritual service of worship. And do not be conformed to this world, but be transformed by the renewing of your mind, that you may prove what the will of God is, that which is good and acceptable and perfect."

Abandonment to God is not easy. No Christian can possibly do this by himself. It is only as we realize our helplessness and yield ourselves completely to God that the Holy Spirit is able to work in and through us to accomplish God's will.

Personal spiritual renewal is characterized by a regular intake of God's Word. As we read the Word, the Holy Spirit illuminates our minds with truth. We begin to view life from God's perspective, which enables us to discern God's will in given situations.

The renewed life is characterized by discipline in prayer. Prayer is our access to God. Through prayer we can unlock God's plan of economy, move heaven into earth, and have victory in the midst of circumstances. "If you abide in Me, and My words abide in you, ask whatever you wish, and it shall be done for you" (John 15:7).

Prayer begins with God and is impressed upon us by the Holy Spirit. God wants us to pray. He goes to great lengths to motivate us to pray.

Jesus continually withdrew from the crowds to be alone with the Father. If He, who knew no sin, needed to be alone with God, how much greater is our need to do the same.

To be disciplined in prayer, we must put into practice the basic elements of prayer.

First, God commands us to be thankful. Thanksgiving is an expression of gratitude for the gifts and blessings of God. Being thankful is not always easy. It is difficult to remain thankful in every situation. Knowing the truth of Romans 8:28 enables us to gain perspective with regard to this command. "And we know that God causes all things to work together for good to those who love God, to those who are called according to His purpose." As we grasp the truth that God is truly working everything that happens in our lives for good, we will begin thanking Him in every situation.

Being thankful leads to an attitude of praise. "I will bless the Lord at all times; His praise shall continually be in my mouth" (Ps. 34:1). God is worthy of the praises of His people. He is pleased when we spend time in praise and adoration for who He is.

Confession is a necessary element of prayer. We never grow spiritually beyond our need to confess. Our attitude toward sin should be that of the psalmist, "I acknowledged my sin to Thee,/And my iniquity I did not hide;/I said, I will confess my transgressions to the Lord" (Ps. 32:5).

Intercession, the most unselfish aspect of prayer, is expressing concern for the needs and interests of others. In bringing our desires for the people we love to God, we are opening the way for God to influence those for whom we pray.

Faith is the key to renewal. God works in our lives according to our faith. When the disciples asked Jesus what they might do to do His work, He replied, "This is the work of God, that you believe in Him whom He has sent" (John 6:29).

To be recipients of revival, we must come in faith, believing a loving and sovereign God will lead us into renewal. As we trust our Lord, He empowers us to become resources through whom He can work to bring revival in the lives of many persons.

Some of the material in this chapter has been copyrighted by the author and is used by permission.

35

From a State Evangelism Director

RENNIE BERRY

Our life-style is our most clearly definable statement of who we are. Perhaps one of the keenest understandings a single adult in Christ may come to is to see the relationship between what God has done in Christ and what He desires to do in us by example. Second Corinthians 5:17-20 *a* explains it this way: "Therefore if any man is in Christ, he is a new creature; the old things are passed away; behold, new things have come. Now all these things are from God, who reconciled us to Himself through Christ and gave us the ministry of reconciliation; namely, that God was in Christ reconciling the world to Himself, not counting their trespasses against them, and He has committed to us the word of reconciliation. Therefore, we are ambassadors for Christ as though God were entreating through us."

The strength of our life-style example is enhanced, not by methods, but by the integrity of the message. Consider if you will the apparent failure in the lives of many Christians to understand what it means to be a new creation and to be free and to be full of Christ's love—clearly reconcilers! When there is interaction between man and God through Christ, there exists the dynamic of, initially, recreation and, continually, renewal. There are attempts on the part of man to be renewed or recreated in another man's image. But there is never freedom; nor is there a joy in being conformed to someone else's life-style. For us who are reconciled to God, the overwhelming joy in living out this life is to be continually renewed in our recreation in Christ. It seems to be at that point that the dynamic of freedom takes over, a revitalizing, "reviving" freedom!

Jesus said in John 8:31 *b*-32, "If you abide in My word, then you are truly disciples of Mine; and you shall know the truth, and the truth shall make you free." He was, of course, referring to Himself (John 14:6 and 8:36). That freedom from guilt and the trappings of man-made legalism is the freedom to become who He wants us to be, is an opportunity to have a life-style which is in the process of being conformed to the likeness of Christ. We must deal with the model of Jesus' life-style of freedom. Because He was the absolute integrity of truth and love, He was free to be a friend of sinners; and they loved Him. It was the religious interpreters of the laws who could not tolerate His freedom to minister in reconciliation.

A conscious decision to develop a life-style of integrity is not the only point. Many single adult Christians today seem to have prioritized a life-style above reproach, whereas more singles need to discover that the question is the conscious determined heart willing to be spent with joy because the love of Jesus leaves no other choice. When we consider what is right or wrong with "eating and drinking" we discover differences. But when we consider Jesus we can only recognize our place in the Son, "Christ in you, the hope of glory" (Col. 1:27b). The matter of being "freed up" to live out a reviving message through the example of our own life-style stands clear and uncomplicated in these words from Galatians 5:1,4,6b, "It is for freedom that Christ has set us free. Stand firm, then, and do not let yourselves be burdened again by a yoke of slavery. . . . You who are trying to be justified by law have been alienated from Christ; you have fallen away from grace. . . . The only thing that counts is faith expressing itself through love" (NIV).

Let us look at a network in which singles have opportunity to apply this freedom in Christ. Second Timothy 1:7 reminds us, "For God has not given us a spirit of timidity, but of power and love and discipline." A life full of love, quietly controlled by the power of the Spirit of God, is quite an acceptable message among those with whom we mingle when we are jogging, playing racquetball, going to lunch, joining co-workers for a time of refreshment after a long day, attending the office Christmas party, taking food to a neighbor. How can we hope to convey the message of reconciliation if we are not willing to call Zacchaeus, a religious outcast, down from the tree and say we want to spend some time with him? Why should we fear the possibility of putting ourselves in a position of compromise? We have been given the spirit of discipline. What better statement could we make to a world full of single adults who are not yet recreated than "I care about you," thus earning the right to be heard. "Christ in you, the hope of glory" gives us the capacity to be authentic, to make ourselves

169

vulnerable, to accept a person as he or she is, to be willing to love, to be willing to go where they are, and to invite them into our homes.

When we consider Jesus, when we give by choice our consecration of will to Him and determine in our innermost being to become like Him, we discover a capacity to be spent with joy because we have been sent by love. "Therefore, we are ambassadors for Christ, as though God were entreating through us" (2 Cor. 5:20). Oh, that God would inspire a revival through our life-style example!

36

From a National Consultant With Singles

DAN R. CRAWFORD

The time in which we live is an unusual time. Young adults are choosing not to marry until later in life or perhaps not at all. Family breakdown and liberal laws allow divorce figures to be at an all-time high. Job stress and the drive to succeed cause many early deaths among men, leaving an unparalleled number of widows. These and a multitude of other complex factors lead to a society that rushes toward one-half of its adult population being single.

Likewise we live in a time that needs revival and is, in fact, ripe for revival. As winds of Spirit-led revival blow across other parts of this world, we desperately need them to blow on us. All God's people are in need of spiritual awakening and genuine renewal. So what are our options?

We can *ignore the time.* Like some misled wino, we can get intoxicated on our own spiritual homebrew to the point that we pass out, hoping that when we awake, all the problems will be gone and life will be perfect. That is not what Paul had in mind when he wrote, "Do not get drunk with wine . . . but be filled with the Spirit" (Eph. 5:18). Some prefer to move through the time with blinders on their eyes, oblivious to the real world around them. Their attitude is, "As long as me and mine get ours, the rest of the world can go on its merry way." This is a tragic option, especially when it invades the church.

A second option is to *reflect back on another time.* Living in the past is always a live option, and there are always significant numbers who choose to do so. Although the good news is the same today as it was yesterday, society has changed. Yesterday's methods may not reach today's people. The secure feeling of proven methods and the desire to relive yesterday's successes are dangerous options, but many churches have chosen that danger rather than risking the dangers of living in the present.

A third option is to *dream of a future time.* While there is nothing wrong with dreams or with projecting the future hope, God never intended for His people to live in the future. Living with a future hope and living in the future may well present two separate life-styles. There are those in our society who prefer to view the present as just a trend, a passing fad. They believe that everything is going to be better tomorrow. It may well be better tomorrow, but that should not serve as an excuse to take today off. In the church, this often translates as hoping that Jesus will return soon and remove us from this present world. He will do so; but until He does, we still have a commission, and it is in the present tense.

The fourth option is to *redeem the time.* God would have us learn from our past as well as plan for our future, but He would also have us live in our present. Whether we like the time or dislike the time; whether we approve of the time or disapprove of the time; whether we're encouraged by the time or discouraged by the time, it is our time. Yesterday—complete with both success and failure—is gone. Tomorrow—complete with both hope and fear—is not yet here. We have this time—a single adult time. Be found "making the most of your time" (Eph. 5:16).

Whether you are a single adult, a minister with single adults, a concerned church leader, a family member with a single adult, or a casual reader, I pray that this book has helped you see that the single adults are significant and deserving recipients of revival. But more than this, I pray that this book has helped you see Christian single adults as possibly the greatest resource for revival in our time.

37

From a Denominational Leader

WILLIAM G. TANNER

This planet is now regarded by many not as a manageable spaceship, but as a terminally ill patient confined to "intensive care." Certainly we are living in an eroding culture. At whatever angle we view our society, we see the edges flaking off. Socially, economically, politically, and spiritually, we witness disturbing signs of decay and deterioration.

The threats of nuclear war have made global holocaust a "live possibility."

Economic uncertainties perplex and upset us; inflation and deflation and stagnation sap and sag our pocketbooks and our purpose; unemployment robs our people of the pleasure of honest work.

New forms of paganism are rising to fill religious vacuums. We worship "unknown gods" and gods we know too well: materialism, comfort, security, stability.

The pattern of these interrelated dangers can intimidate the church and paralyze its initiative for world evangelism, or these dangers can be the greatest alarm clock in history, awakening the sleeping church to its fundamental role of bringing about the "kingdom on earth, as in heaven."

The very urgency of the situation should drive Southern Baptists to make sacrifices necessary for the greatest missionary outreach ever attempted.

After all, it's no more a sacrifice for us than it was for the early church. Those first Christians had far less "potential" than we: no great or untapped wealth, no amazingly elaborate communications networks, no acceptance by authorities. Their zeal and their serious commitment sent the "church growth line" zooming off the charts.

Today our land staggers between Vanity Fair and Armageddon. While we launch to the stars, we mire down in the slime of our age. And the irony is this: Unless there is a spiritual awakening, our scientific accomplishments will exceed our moral ones.

For we simply are not getting the gospel message to our nation. We have more ways of telling the story than ever before, yet one hundred million people do not belong to any congregation!

We talk a good game. But every time we face the necessity of actually, personally being "on mission for Christ," thousands of us stampede to the sidelines. Noninvolvement is the order of the day.

We need more than a spectator mentality. The greatest tragedy of the twentieth century is not that we Christians are deficient in money, knowledge, methods, facilities, training, leaders, or pulpit eloquence. Our greatest tragedy is that we have neglected and almost forgotten the power that is available to us through the Holy Spirit.

We want revivals without repentance, souls without sacrifice, getting without giving, ruling without serving, living without dying to self.

In our quest for ease and acceptance we have established such good terms with this world that we have forgotten our mission to be a voice from another world: a heavenly world of caring, of loving; a world of peace and concern; a world of promise and of hope; a world of forgiveness, of grace.

Our outposts from God's world remain our churches.

Christ meant His following, the church, to be a power for good in the war against evil. He instituted the church not to be a mutual admiration society. Rather the church is here to change the world; its business is not to preserve the status quo or perpetuate the past, but to provide a redemptive answer for the sin that festers like a cancer in the soul of humankind.

Christ was not decorating society when he organized the church; he was developing an attack force. The church's role is to be active, not passive; to be involved, not isolated. And our Savior's promise is that we will not fight alone. The church is not a besieged city, surrounded by the world's evils. Don't we, after all, believe the church is a marching army with a Commander who cannot be conquered, a gospel which cannot be stilled, a battle plan which ensures victory?

Maybe it's time we practiced what we've preached. All over our nation millions of single adults are waiting for us to tell them that

Jesus Christ and His church are here for them, too. Whether they have that good news depends, finally, on you and on me.

Bibliography

The author, though recommending the following books to assist the reader in the Christian growth process, does not necessarily endorse all contents of the books listed. The discerning reader is urged to be alert to books written from a totally Christian perspective and those that are not.

This bibliography is arranged with the several categories of singleness in mind as well as the person who begins and builds a ministry among singles in the local church in a leadership capacity.

Never-Married Singles

Allbritton, Cliff. *How to Get Married and Stay That Way.* Nashville: Broadman Press, 1982.

Anders, Sarah Frances. *Woman Alone: Confident and Creative.* Nashville: Broadman Press, 1976.

Bradley, Buff, et al. *Single: Living Your Own Way.* Redding, Massachusetts: Addison-Wesley Publishing Co., 1977.

Brock, Raymond T. *Dating and Waiting for Marriage.* Springfield, Missouri: Gospel Publishing House, 1982.

Cargan, Leonard and Melko, Matthew. *Singles.* Beverly Hills, California: Sage, 1982.

Clarkson, Margaret. *So You're Single.* Wheaton, Illinois: Harold Shaw Publishers, 1978.

Collins, Gary R. *It's O.K. to Be Single.* Waco: Word, 1976.

Edwards, Marie. *The Challenge of Being Single.* Los Angeles: J. P. Tarcher, 1972.

Evening, Margaret. *Who Walk Alone—A Consideration of the Single Life.* London: Hodder and Stoughton, 1974.

McAllaster, Elva Arlie. *Free to Be Single.* 1st ed. Chappaqua, New York: Christian Herald Books, 1979.

McConnell, Adeline. *Single After Fifty.* New York: McGraw-Hill, 1978.

Miller, Keith. *The Single Experience.* Waco: Word Books, 1981.

Salter, Debbie. *One Is More Than Un.* Grand Rapids: Baker Book House, 1979.

Smith, Leon and Smith, Antoinette. *Preparing for Christian Marriage.* Nashville: Abingdon, 1982.

Sproul, R. C. *Discovering the Intimate Marriage.* St. Louis: Bethany, 1981.

Swindoll, Luci. *Wide My World, Narrow My Bed.* Portland, Oregon: Multnomah, 1982.

Towns, Jim. *One Is Not a Lonely Number.* Dallas: Crescendo Press, 1977.

Yates, Martha. *Coping: A Survival Manual for Women Alone.* Englewood Cliffs: Prentice Hall, 1976.

Yoder, Bruce and Imo Leanne Yoder. *Single Voices.* Scottsdale, Pennsylvania: Herald Press, 1982.

Divorced

Arnold, William V. *When Your Parents Divorce.* Philadelphia: Westminster Press, 1980.

Besson, Clyde Colvin. *Picking Up the Pieces.* Millford, Michigan: Mott Media, 1982.

Buchanan, Neal C., and Chamberlain, Eugene. *Helping Children of Divorce.* Nashville: Broadman Press, 1981.

Crook, Roger H. *An Open Book to the Christian Divorcee.* Nashville: Broadman Press, 1974.

Dahl, Gerald J. *Why Christian Marriages Are Breaking Up.* Nashville: Thomas Nelson, 1979.

Eisler, Riane. *Dissolution: No-Fault Divorce, Marriage, and the Future of Women.* New York City: McGraw-Hill, 1977.

Hensley, J. Clark. *Coping with Being Single Again.* Nashville: Broadman Press, 1978.

Hosier, Helen Kosiman. *The Other Side of Divorce.* New York City: Hawthorn Books, 1975.

Hudson, Lofton R. *Is This Divorce Really Necessary?* Nashville: Broadman, 1983.

Krantzle, Mel. *Creative Divorce: A New Opportunity for Personal Growth.* New York City: M. Evans & Co., 1973.

Kysar, Myrna. *The Asundered: Biblical Teachings on Divorce and Remarriage.* Atlanta: John Knox Press, 1978.

Laney, Carl L. *The Divorce Myth.* St. Louis: Bethany House, 1981.

Lovette, C. S. *The Compassionate Side of Divorce.* Old Tappan: Fleming H. Revell, 1975.

Peppler, Alice Stolper. *Divorce and Christian.* St. Louis: Concordia, 1974.

Salk, Lee. *What Every Child Would Like Parents to Know About Divorce.* New York City: Harper and Row, 1978.

Shahan, Lynn. *Living Alone and Liking It.* Beverly Hills: Stratford Press, 1981.

Shepard, Morris A. *Divorced Dads: Their Kids, Ex-wives, and New Lives.* New York City: Berkley Books, 1979.

Small, Dwight H. *The Right to Remarry.* Old Tappan: Fleming H. Revell Company, 1975. Accompanying cassette.

Smoke, Jim. *Growing Through Divorce.* Irvine, California: Harvest House, 1976.

Towner, Jason. *Jason Loves Jane.* Nashville: Benson, 1979.

Wallerstein, Judith S. *Surviving the Breakup: How Children and Parents Cope with Divorce.* New York City: Basic Books, Inc., 1980.

Westburg, Granger. *Good Grief.* Philadelphia: Fortress Press, 1971.

Woodson, Les. *Divorce and the Gospel of Grace.* Waco: Word Books, 1979.

Leadership

Brown, Raymond K. *Reach Out to Singles: A Challenge To Ministry.* Philadelphia: Westminster Press, 1979.

Buchanan, Neal C., and Chamberlain, Eugene. *Helping Children of Divorce.* Nashville: Broadman Press, 1981.

Christoff, Nicholas B. *Saturday Night, Sunday Morning.* New York City: Harper and Row, 1978.

Cole, W. Douglas. *Wants Vs. Shoulds.* Nashville: Convention Press, 1980.

Collins, Gary R. *It's O.K. to Be Single.* Waco: Word, 1976.

Craig, Floyd A. *How to Communicate with Single Adults.* Nashville: Broadman Press, 1978.

Dow, Robert Arthur. *Ministry with Single Adults.* Valley Forge: Judson Press, 1977.

Drakeford, John W. *Experiential Bible Study.* Nashville: Broadman Press, 1974.

Hugen, Walter D. *The Church's Ministry to the Older Unmarried.* Grand Rapids: William B. Eerdmans, 1960.

Kerr, Horace. *How to Minister to Senior Adults in Your Church.* Nashville: Broadman, 1980.

Lawson, Linda. *Working with Single Adults in Sunday School.* Nashville: Convention Press, 1978.

Lyon, William. *A Pew for One, Please.* New York City: Seabury Press, 1977.

May, Carl. *You Can Do It!* Nashville: Broadman Press, 1977.

Miller, Keith, and Miller, Andrea Wells. *Faith, Intimacy, and Risk in the Single Life.* Waco: Word Inc., 1980.

Potts, Nancy D. *Counseling with Single Adults.* Nashville: Broadman Press, 1978.

Scroggs, James R. *Letting Love In.* Englewood Cliffs: Prentice-Hall, Inc., 1978.

Sessoms, Robert. *150 Ideas for Activities with Senior Adults.* Nashville: Broadman, 1977.

Simenauer, Jacqueline, and David, Carrol. *Singles.* NY: Simon and Shuster, 1982.

Simon, Sidney. *Caring, Feeling, Touching.* Niles, Illinois: Argus, 1976.

Smith, Ann Alexander. *How to Start a Single Adult Ministry.* Nashville: Sunday School Board of the Southern Baptist Convention.

Smith, Ann Alexander. *Divorce Adjustment Workshop: A Guide for Leaders.* Nashville: Sunday School Board of the Southern Baptist Convention.

Towns, Jim. *Solo Flight.* Wheaton, Illinois: Tyndale House Publishers, 1980.

Wood, Britton. *Single Adults Want to be the Church, Too.* Nashville: Broadman Press, 1977.

Middle Years

Barks, Herb. *Prime Time.* Nashville: Thomas Nelson, 1978.

Conway, Jim. *Men In Mid-Life Crisis.* Elgin, Illinois: David C. Cook Publishing Co., 1978.

Donohugh, Donald. *The Middle Years.* Philadelphia: Saunders Press, 1981.

Hulme, William E. *Mid-Life Crises.* Philadelphia: Westminster, 1980.

Madden, Myron and Mary Ben. *The Time of Your Life.* Nashville: Broadman Press, 1977.

McConnell, Adeline. *Single After Fifty.* New York City: McGraw-Hill, 1980.

Rubin, Lillian B. *Women of a Certain Age: The Midlife Search for Self.* New York City: Harper and Row, 1979.

Personal Growth

Couey, Richard. *Lifelong Fitness and Fulfillment.* Nashville: Broadman Press, 1980.

Dickson, Elaine. *Say No, Say Yes to Change.* Nashville: Broadman, 1982.

Duncan, James E. *The Reason for Joy.* Nashville: Broadman, 1978.

Dyer, Wayne W. *Your Erroneous Zones.* New York City: Funk & Wagnalls, 1977.

Eareckson, Joni. *Joni.* Grand Rapids: Zondervan, 1978.

Galloway, Dale. *How to Feel Like Somebody Again.* Irvine, California: Harvest House, 1978.

George, Jeanette Clift. *Some Run with Feet of Clay.* Old Tappan: Revell, 1978.

Hayner, Jerry. *God's Best to You.* Nashville: Broadman, 1982.

Hayner, Jerry. *Say Hello to Life.* Nashville: Broadman, 1980.

Hollis, Harry, Jr. *Thank God for Sex.* Nashville: Broadman, 1975.

Hunter, John E. *Jesus Speaks Today.* Nashville: Broadman Press, 1982.

Keller, W. Phillip. *Taming Tensions.* Grand Rapids: Baker Book House, 1979.

Lester, Andrew. *Sex Is More Than a Word.* Nashville: Broadman, 1973.

Miller, Keith. *The Becomers.* Waco: Word Books, 1973.

Newman, Mildred and Berkowitz, Bernard. *How To Be Your Own Best Friend.* New York City: Random House, 1971.

Parrino, John J. *From Panic to Power: The Positive Use of Stress.* New York City: John Wiley, 1979.

Poinsett, Brenda. *Prayerfully Yours.* Nashville: Broadman, 1979.

Powell, John. *He Touched Me.* Niles, Illinois: Argus Communications, 1974.

Powell, John. *Fully Human, Fully Alive.* Niles, Illinois: Argus, 1976.

Rubin, David. *Everything You Always Wanted to Know About Nutrition.* New York City: Simon and Schuster, 1978.

Salter, Debbie. *One is More Than Un: A Personal Growth Book for the Single Adult.* Kansas City: Beacon Hill Press of Kansas City, 1978.

Selye, Hans. *Stress Without Distress.* New York City: Signet, 1974.

Sheehy, Gail. *Passages.* New York City: E. P. Dutton and Company, 1976.

Smith, Charles E. *Commitment: The Cement of Love.* Nashville: Broadman Press, 1982.

Stephens, Shirley. *A New Testament View of Women.* Nashville: Broadman, 1982.

Steebeck, Mary, ed. *Single . . . But Not Alone.* Nashville: JM Publications, 1982.

Towns, Jim. *Singles Alive.* Pelican Press, 1984.

Towns, Jim. *My Life: Joy in Being.* Nashville: Convention Press, 1981.

Vetter, Bob and June. *Jesus Was a Single Adult.* Elgin, Illinois: David C. Cook, 1978.

Welch, Reuben. *We Really Do Need Each Other.* Nashville: Impact Books, n.p.d.

Separation

Chapman, Gary. *Hope for the Separated.* Chicago: Moody Press, 1982.

Gatby, Richard H. *Single Father's Handbook: A Guide for Separated and Divorced Fathers.* Garden City, New York: Anchor Books, 1979.

Oates, Wayne Edward. *Pastoral Care and Counseling in Grief and Separation.* Philadelphia: Fortress, 1976.

Rowlands, Peter. *Saturday Parent: A Book for Separated Families.* New York City: Continuum, 1980.

Vahanian, Tilla. Separation; Coping with the breakup of a marriage. [Tape Recording.] Lessons for Living, division of Mass Communications, Inc., 1976.

Weiss, Robert. *Marital Separation.* New York City: Basic Books, 1975.

Single Parents

Briggs, Dorothy Corkille. *Your Child's Self-Esteem.* Garden City, New York: Doubleday, 1970.

Chandler, Linda S. *David Asks "Why?"* Nashville: Broadman Press, 1982.

Coleman, Lucien. *How to Prepare Your Child for Marriage.* Nashville: Convention Press, 1978.

Duvall, Evelyn M. *Evelyn Duvall's Handbook for Parents.* Nashville: Broadman, 1974.

Elder, Carl A. *Values and Moral Development in Children.* Nashville: Broadman, 1976.

Gardner, Richard A. *A Parent's Book About Divorce.* Doubleday, 1977.

Gordon, Thomas. *Parent Effectiveness Training, A Tested Way to Raise Responsible Children.* New York City: Peter Wyden, 1970.

Grant, Wayne. *Growing Parents Growing Children.* Nashville: Convention, 1978.

Grant, Wayne. *Discipline in the Christian Home.* Nashville: Convention Press, 1975.

Hope, Karol, and Young, Nancy, eds. *Momma: The Source Book for Single Mothers.* New York City: Polub Books, 1976.

Howell, John C. *You and Your Retarded Child.* St. Louis: Concordia House, 1974.

Schlesinger, Benjamin. *The One-Parent Family, Perspectives and Annotated Bibliography,* 3rd ed. Toronto: University of Toronto Press, 1975.

Shrum, David. *Creating Love and Warmth for Our Children.* Nashville: Broadman, 1977.

Smith, Charles. *Helps for the Single-Parent Christian Family.* Nashville: Convention Press, 1978. An accompanying teaching tape is also available.

Watts, Virginia. *The Single Parent.* Old Tappan: Revell, 1976.

Weiss, Robert. *Going It Alone: The Family and Social Situation of the Single Parent.* New York City: Basic Books, 1979.

Stepparenting

Berman, Claire. *Making It as a Stepparent: New Roles/New Rules.* New York City: Doubleday, 1980.

Capaldi, F. *Stepfamilies: A Cooperative Responsibility.* Viewpoints-Vision Books, 1979.

Lofas, Jeannette and Ruth Roosevelt. *Living In Step.* New York City: Stein and Day, 1976.

Ricci, Tsolina. *Mom's House/Dad's House: Making Shared Custody Work.* New York City: Macmillan, 1980.

Satir, Virginia. *Peoplemaking.* Palo Alto: Science and Behavior Books, 1972.

Visher, Emily and John. *How to Win as a Stepfamily.* New York City: Dembner Books, 1982.

Wallerstein, Judith S., and Kelly, Joan B. *Surviving the Breakup.* New York City: Basic Books, 1980.

Wooley, Persia. *The Custody Handbook.* New York City: Simon and Schuster, 1980.

Widowed

Bogard, David. *Valleys and Vistas: After Losing Life's Partner.* Grand Rapids: Baker Book House, 1974.

Brite, Mary. *Triumph Over Tears.* Nashville: Thomas Nelson, 1979.

Brooks, D. P. *Dealing with Death—A Christian Perspective.* Nashville: Broadman Press, 1974.

Brown, Velma Darbo. *After Weeping, A Song.* Nashville: Broadman Press, 1980.

Caine, Lynn. *Widow.* New York City: William Morrow, 1974.

Fabisch, Judith. *Not Ready to Walk Alone.* Grand Rapids: Zondervan, 1978.

Hensley, J. Clark. *Coping with Being Single Again.* Nashville: Broadman Press, 1978.

Kohn, Jane Burgess and Willard K. *The Widower.* Boston: Beacon Press, 1978.

Levine, James A. *Who Will Raise the Children?—New Options for Fathers (and Mothers)* Philadelphia: Lippincott, 1976.

Nye, Miriam Baker. *But I Never Thought He'd Die.* Philadelphia: Westminster Press, 1978.

Peterson, James A. and Briley, Michael L. *Widows and Widowhood.* Chicago: Follett Publishing Company, 1977.

Stevens, Velma Darbo. *A Fresh Look at Loneliness.* Nashville: Broadman Press, 1981.

Towns, Jim. *Growing Through Grief.* Warner Press, 1984.

Evangelism Among Single Adults

Aldrich, Joseph C. *Lifestyle Evangelism.* Portland: Multnomah Press, 1981.

Bailey, Waylon. *As You Go: Foundations for Evangelism.* New Orleans: Insight Press, 1981.

Brestin, Dee. *Finders Keepers.* Wheaton, Illinois: Shaw Publishing Co., 1983.

Coleman, Robert E. *The Master Plan of Evangelism.* Westwood, New Jersey: Fleming H. Revell, 1963, 1964.

Crawford, Dan R. *EvangeLife: A Guide to Life-style Evangelism.* Nashville: Broadman Press, 1984.

Ford, Leighton. *Good News Is for Sharing.* Elgin, Illinois: David C. Cook, 1977.

Henrichsen, Walter A. *Disciples Are Made Not Born.* Wheaton, Illinois: Victor Books, 1974.

Innes, Dick. *I Hate Witnessing.* Ventura, California: Vision Press, 1983.

Johnson, Ron, Hinkle, Joseph W., and Lowry, Charles. *Oikos: A Practical Approach to Family Evangelism.* Nashville: Broadman Press, 1982.

Little, Paul E. *How to Give Away Your Faith.* Downers Grove, Illinois: Inter-Varsity Press, 1966.

McDill, Wayne. *Making Friends for Christ.* Nashville: Broadman Press, 1979.

McPhee, Arthur. *Friendship Evangelism.* Grand Rapids: Zondervan, 1978.

Miles, Delos. *Introduction to Evangelism.* Nashville: Broadman Press, 1983.

Miles, Delos. *Master Principles of Evangelism.* Nashville: Broadman Press, 1982.

Moore, Waylon. *Multiplying Disciples.* Colorado Springs: Navpress, 1981.

Neighbor, Ralph W., Jr., and Thomas, Calvin. *Target Group Evangelism.* Nashville: Broadman Press, 1975.

Petersen, Jim. *Evangelism as a Lifestyle.* Colorado Springs: Navpress, 1980.

Pippert, Rebecca Manley. *Out of the Salt Shaker into the World.* Downers Grove, Illinois: Inter-Varsity Press, 1979.

Rinker, Rosalind. *You Can Witness with Confidence.* Grand Rapids: Zonder-
  van, 1962.
Thompson, W.   *Concentric Circles of Concern.* Nashville: Broadman
  Press, 1981.

90158